SUSTAINABLE LIFE
The New Success

Nature's Wisdom for Sustainable You, Sustainable Work,
Sustainable Love, Sustainable World and Future

James Wanless, Ph.D.

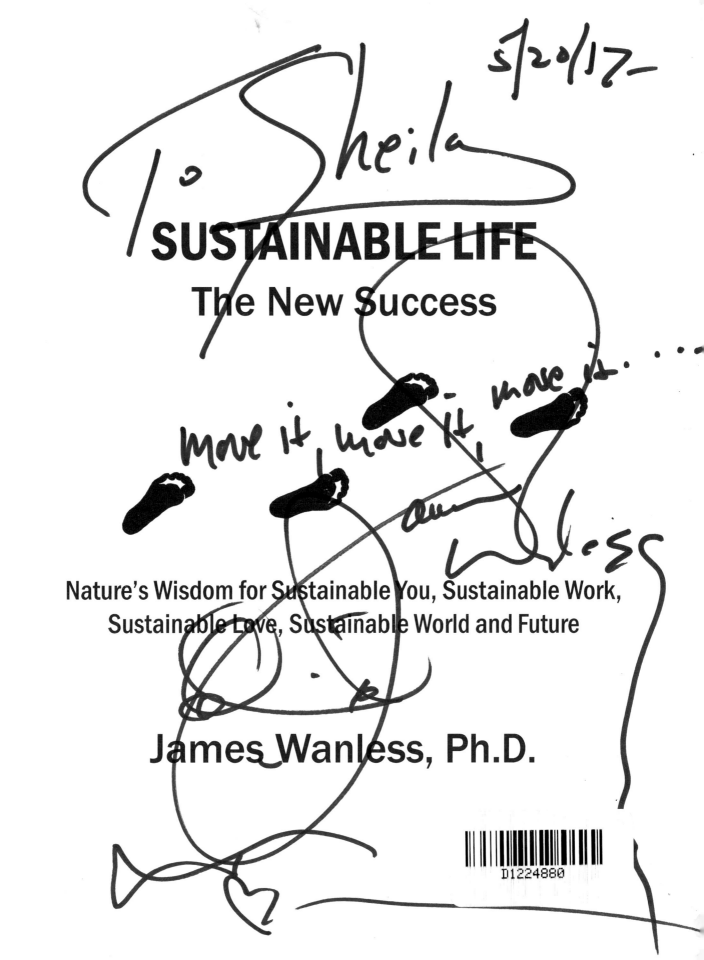

Sustainable Life: The New Success
James Wanless, Ph.D.
ISBN: 978-0-9833024-8-3

Published by The Living Future,
A Cigno E Gallo, Inc. Company.
San Francisco, California USA
www.TheLivingFuture.org

Card photomontages for the Sustain Yourself Cards created by
James Wanless, Ph.D. Published by Tarot Media Company.
This Deck of 101 eco-principles is a useful tool and companion for living the Sustainable Life.
www.SustainYourselfCards.com

Book and Card border design by Chris Lowrance Illustration + Design
Typefaces used: Palatino LT, Franklin Gothic

For a schedule of Sustainability events with James Wanless, please visit the website at
www.TheLivingFuture.org

For more of James' work on Sustainability, please visit the wesbite at
www.SustainYourselfCards.com

Contents

Preface

Sustainability is a vital sign of life. To live well and live long, sustainability is the way. In fact, it's the way of life. Sustainable life means living well and living long. To do this requires living whole — which means to stay healthy, be happy, grow wise, have sufficient material wealth, be creative, adaptable and resilient, preserve the earth, contribute to community and social harmony — all in a conscious and balanced way.

The single most significant change in recent human history is that we live longer and longer. Whether you are young, middle-aged, or retiring, you have a way to go. And we all want to have a quality life that gets better and better. Sustainability is about living a healthy, happy, and wealthy (enough) life, and it's not easy. Life is demanding and changing, and to maintain we have to keep up and keep going.

Sustainability is the "new success," because it's sustainable success, and it's not a given. It's an ability—the "sustain-ability"—that needs to be learned and exercised. Sustainable life skills are primordial, but have been reintroduced as imperatives into modern life by amazing studies from the emergent sciences that are biological, environmental, social, evolutionary, psychological, quantum, metaphysical, and neurological.

The most valuable source of sustainability is you—the sustain-ability of optimizing all of you, the number one resource. Learning from nature, the greatest living model and mentor of sustainability, you cannot afford to deplete, waste, or poison yourself. Tap your natural creative mind, your emotional power and intelligence, your renewable body, and your life-force spirit. You will do no less than realize your vast human potential.

Sustainability is not just about health or wealth. It's about healthy everything, because everything affects everything. It's having a whole and balanced life of loving relationships and partnerships, living in your place on Earth, doing passionate and productive work, and caring for the future.

There is no particular way or form to follow. It's the energy behind whatever you do that sustains you the most. Follow the energy, the bottom line. Live energetically, mindfully; surf your emotions and act on your intuitive impulses, recharge with an energy diet, and move to the life-force energy, the "inner chi," to your destined life.

In this age of rapid change, adapt and be change-able. If you are not busy changing, you are busy dying. Know how to recycle and renew your life—restore, redefine, recover, restart, and "re" again. I learned firsthand how to recycle my life because a few years ago, at age sixty-five, I became more vulnerable to the vagaries of some ill health, suffered financial setbacks and a deteriorating work situation, moved to a city, and had a major relationship shift. I was forced to rebound and reinvent my life, and thus began my search for how to keep living well and long.

Riding the cycle of resilience and perpetual renewal, you naturally get creative. With so much "new and different" every day, creative living is a must. Be imaginative, go forth adventurously, and master the means to manifest the wondrous magic of creation.

To sustain is not a sprint to accumulation. It's a path of life and earth talk. Keep your footprint light but leave a legacy – your footprint that serves and guides others – and keep going.

What I've discovered is that the sustain-abilities are innate, but they must be expressed and exercised for them to work. Apply nature's great sustainability wisdom of "use it or lose it." All of these abilities are do-able: do them, and sustain on.

Part One:
SUSTAINABILITY MAP, MOTIVATION, MENTOR

Every successful endeavor starts out with some kind of road map. The sustainability map becomes clear as we explore what sustainability means as the "new success." But maps never get us anywhere unless we take action, and this requires motivation. As we shall see, there are plenty of reasons and even imperatives for activating the map. A guiding mentor—whether it's a GPS, coach, or wise friend—always helps on the journey. The sustainability process and adventure has a mentor ready for us for all occasions, a sage that always surrounds us and dwells within us: nature. By connecting with nature, and with our own nature, we tap directly into the map for the new success.

1: The New Success

My exploration of sustainable living has led me to a new and deeper meaning of success. In today's world, the traditional measures of success have evolved. We want more than just to be well off; we want to enjoy well-being in all ways— we want to be happy, healthy, wealthy, wise, and more, and to sustain it all for a long life. Because we have materially progressed in life, we want more and expect more. We have raised the bar as we seek an enduring and continuously rich quality of life.

The new success of sustainability is not measured by numbers or quantity. It's not about how much money you have or how long you've been married or how many miles you run. The sustainable life is more intrinsic—it's about how you feel, and how whole and renewable you are for the long term. This is what we're seeing in the world now as countries begin to measure their quality of life, moving from the economic-based gross domestic product, or GDP, and income to GNH, gross national happiness.

It's not enough just to attain a happy, high-quality life; we must be able to sustain it, and that means we must be change-able. The new success is "sustainable success," which is different from success as it's been defined in the past, because it's renewable. The game changer of what it means to be successful now is change itself. Just because we've achieved some success, there is no guarantee now that we'll have it forever.

Because we want the complete and renewable life, we must approach it in a holistic way. This is a fundamental principle for the new success. The more we want, the more is required of us—our mind, heart, body, spirit, all applied to

our love life, relationships of all kinds, business endeavors, social communities, and natural environment. It's a lot. Sustainability can, indeed, be exhausting and consuming. The secret is how to keep going, and it's found within the "sustain-abilities."

The sustain-abilities are the key to twenty-first century life, and if you follow them, your success is not only renewable, but you are also renewable. In the sustain-abilities, you find the formula to achieve and realize success in the first place. Because it's all sustainable, real, and lasting, you have the new success.

Sustainability is more meaningful and expansive than traditional success—it's "the way of life," a kind of spiritual path and philosophy to cultivate and conserve the life-force that creates us. Sustainability is an evolutionary lifestyle because it requires that we consciously create and grow ourselves as human beings and produce a legacy through which ongoing generations can prosper and develop.

2: The Sustainability Imperative

Though we have experienced many social, economic, and technological advances, life is more challenging than ever. We are experiencing the speeding up of change, unpredictable swings of interconnected economic dislocations and depressions, mushrooming populations, mind-boggling complexities, confrontational politics and relationships, polarized society, divisive inequalities, new types of mental and physical pathologies, heightened expectations of everything, and so many choices to make about all of these things. As a result, we are uncertain, we are anxious, we are overwhelmed, we are stressed, we are sick, we are run down, we are crazed. Though we live longer, we are probably less healthy and work harder. Despite economic growth, we have lost real wealth in many cases. We now have less sense of community and family with an ever-widening social and generational gap. Over all of this looms an unbalanced natural environment at risk.

Because of my own experience of these uncertain and vexing conditions, I set out to be sustain-able. My meager social security check hasn't exactly eased me into retirement; in fact, I've been propelled into "refirement." So, now here I am, almost seventy, working more and working differently, still trying to figure out my taxes and phone plan, encountering the trials and tribulations of twenty-first century dating, learning the changing nuances of Facebook, being called old and yet feeling young, and in some ways, just getting started.

All these incongruities and hardships are only inconveniences and annoyances. They are symptoms, however, of deeper perils—depletion, waste of human resources, and toxic behavior—that challenge the very future of humankind. I think humans are an endangered species. Why? Because we don't live like nature, and we don't acknowledge that we are part of nature. Unlike the rest of the natural world, we deplete, waste, and poison. And we have enormous power. We are the greatest danger on Earth. We are, at once, one of the most threatened species and at the same time the most threatening life form. We are the greatest planetary resource, and we are squandering all our resources. We are the most powerful agent on Earth and we are the most toxic. The most unsustainable ecological disaster waiting to happen in Earth's biosphere is the human being.

Depletion

We exhaust and deplete ourselves not only because of our lifestyles but because we don't tap the renewable sources of energy within us. Energy is the bottom line of sustainability. Yet, we don't think in terms of energy as part of living. We run down our bodies and our brains because we are not energy efficient, and we do not know how to generate and regenerate ourselves. When we are young, we take energy for granted, but even now, the young as well as the aged are wearing down under the pressures of modern life.

Whether it's a young person looking for work or changing from job to job, or a single mother, a middle-aged couple facing unemployment and debt, a retiring baby boomer looking for a meaningful livelihood, or a sick person facing medical costs and a life of loneliness, the essential sustain-ability is to keep going without going under.

"Re" Yourself

The new success is to be sustain-able, so the holy grail of today is to renew and re-renew – to "re." The challenge and opportunity in this 21st century is to "re"—refresh our minds and re-energize our bodies, recover and rebound from setbacks, rejuvenate emotionally, restart projects, reawaken creativity, repurpose life, reinvent work, retool and relearn skills, rekindle relationships, retreat and recess

Self-Creation

Cells

from situations, recuperate from wounds, rebalance finances, renegotiate agreements—re, re, re. Knowing how to be resilient, how to regenerate and recycle ourselves is the medicine and magic for this topsy-turvy world.

The single most effective way to "re" your life is to follow the "life-force," the creative energy and prime mover that brings us into being and sustains us. Call this spirit, god, mystery, the almighty, or whatever you like; there is some ineffable source of life that is the renewable supply of energy. To harness this power, exercise all parts of yourself to channel the life-force impulse, which is that something that turns us on emotionally, fires up the imagination, gets the heart pumping in the body, and inspires action. Move to what motivates you from moment to moment. This is not about thinking, or trying to do something right, or smart, or appropriate, or anything else but what moves you. With energy, anything is possible, especially overcoming mistakes and setbacks. There are, however, some caveats for this energized way of navigating your life, as we shall see in subsequent chapters.

Dedicating my life to this sustainable energy way of being has made me more spontaneous, free, and expressive, all of which has led me to be more creative, productive, and happy. And younger! It's learning to ride the wave, whatever emotion on the ocean of emotion, that gets you going. Don't judge it, ride it! Surf your life to save your life. On this energy path, you will find your own flow and your own wave, which is your authentic way of authoring the life of your greatest heartfelt vision.

Generally, we guide our lives based on an unconscious habit or a mental idea or belief about what we should do. Thus, we are not our true selves and not in our own power. We get depleted. Because we haven't learned the importance of how to "re" ourselves and live energetically, we look for a magic bullet that will pick us up and save us, whether it be an energy drink, a double latte, pill, hormone, miracle, the lottery, or some outside force and "savior" like a company, rich uncle, the government, or a game-changing event. Sometimes it's hope or a fantasy that keeps us going. When all that is exhausted, then what? To be sustain-able is to be responsible (response-able), which is to be "re-able."

This leads us to the next "re-ability"—proper use of inner resources and opportunities.

Waste

It is little wonder that we wear down when it's clear that we are not anywhere near to living up to our optimum capabilities. As a professional in the human potential field, I can assure you that none of us, including me, has a complete understanding about our capacities. Our limited ways of being have become very exposed by twenty-first-century science and by our outdated, counterproductive, habitual behaviors.

Our intellectual and creative genius is compromised by old ways of thinking that are inefficient and not so smart as we believe. We mine our brain like we drill for fossil fuels. Memorization, knowledge of trivia, and robot-like repetition are finite, dead-end uses of our rich and diverse mind. Machines and computers can do that far better. Tapping the immeasurable gift of our right brain for whole-brain creativity is the way of endless, renewable brain power. The real treasure box of modern life is not things but our billions of brain neurons full of calculation and imagination. To live sustainably and abundantly, work the rich goldmine of that three-and-a half-pound soggy, gray object in your skull.

We have underestimated and underutilized the motivational power and intelligence of our heart of our emotions. Few of us live an inspired life, an existence infused with passion and relentless purpose. Our role models and heroes are always those who have been mightily motivated. It seems to me that most of us lack the zeal and drive to exploit the depth and heights of our human being. It's like we've been tranquilized.

Physically, we have become sedentary, which is now officially a pathology called "sedentary behavior disorder." We are sedated by watching the proverbial "bread and circuses" as we become spectators of life instead of participants in life. A spectator society watches the world go by and forge ahead. When we sit at work, in a car, at a meal, in front of a TV, we have automatically lost twenty percent of the oxygen to our brain, and brains require enormous amounts of oxygen to optimally function. The sedentary lifestyle is an oxygen-deprived existence that also produces significant health issues. The body rules, so when it suffers, everything else is stymied and the realization of our dreams remains a fantasy.

We get secure and lazy, and cease growing and stretching ourselves once we have reached a plateau that suffices. I call it "death by comfort." To attain the highest level of a universal and natural growth cycle—which exists throughout nature and in every human endeavor whether it be a relationship, business, organization, or personal life—requires conscious "breakthrough change." Ordinarily we resist such change. Let's face it; we just don't like to change even though it will bring us more fulfillment and reward. And we don't even know how to make changes, primarily because we don't want to be inconvenienced and unsettled by the unknown. We are creatures of habit.

In the workplace, our productivity is curbed because we do not enjoy our jobs. A Gallup poll of a million American workers found that only one in three is happily engaged in their work. What a waste of wo-manpower. (Gallup Employee

Engagement Index. Oct. 28, 2011. http://www.gallup.com/poll/150383/majority-american-workers-not-engaged-jobs.aspx)

Why is it that Silicon Valley has enjoyed such success? Because it's a culture of turned-on, impassioned people on a mission who thus work their tails off and get the most out of themselves.

Fortunately, in my own life, I changed my career track long ago to pursue a profession that excited me and still does; hence, I can sustain, repeat, and not deplete. I can keep honing my skills and developing my craft.

Our so-called developed societies have fragmented and fractured into factionalism. An evolved organization or culture is a collaborative, mutually supportive community, not an ideological, racial, or ethnic battleground, nor one of individualism by accumulative greed. We can only get the most out of ourselves if we live in a social environment that encourages a level playing field of equal opportunity. Diversity, openness, and accessible possibilities are all required for the fulfillment of our human potential.

A sustainable society invests in the future and so is willing to make sacrifices and forgo some immediate gratification. Unfortunately, our education system, a primary engine which creates a sustainable future of growing people, has been neglected and bypassed by the modern world. American education now serves to oppress rather than liberate, to control rather than empower, to test well rather than encourage creativity.

We must each ask ourselves, "What talents have I unused or underused? Where have I underperformed, and how have I undervalued myself?"

Toxicity

We all know that we poison our natural environment and our bodies, but our toxicity all starts in our thinking. It is true about the power of mind—how we think is how we live—so we must look at our mental processes. Negative, closed, critical, defensive, and narrow thinking lead to a noxious life. We are ignorant of the power and poison of our thoughts, which make us fearful, delusional, stressed, and depressed. Becoming aware of our thoughts, as we do in cognitive psychology, we can make headway in clearing and reforming our polluted mental ways.

Though we have evolved into humans through the use of our thinking brain, we have become overly mental—consulting our thoughts for every decision and assessment. The problem is that the logical, thinking faculty of the brain has hijacked other parts of our marvelous mental "sogware." The brilliance of the analytical mind is that it's judgmental: it has the gift of dissection and separation. But this quality has been perverted into a pervasive depiction of everything as right or wrong, good or evil, me or you. It's an "either-or" mentality that divides up everything and everyone, including labeling ourselves as good or bad. Poison kills, and we "kill" ourselves and others with our inner critical judge. This mentality leads to poisonous language that magnifies differences into conflicting and warring camps.

Because we are mostly controlled by our thoughts and identify ourselves with them, these judgments of ourselves and others become hardened into an ego sense of self-identity that must be defended at all costs. This "neanderthink" mindset destroys any sense of our own wholeness and interconnectedness with the world, and pits person against person, tribe against tribe, and human against nature.

Living in this age of awareness, there is hope that the infiltration of cognitive behavior psychology and meditative mindfulness into mainstream understanding will eventually prevail, hopefully before we kill ourselves and others with the sword and shotgun of thoughts as weapons of everyday discourse.

3: Nature Knows How

We can see the issues before us, but do we have solutions? Do we have a mentor who knows how, a model and plan that work, and a vision that is viable to sustain ourselves? Or do we continue to just stumble through?

Like a seed that bears the imprint of promise and potential, sustainable living starts inside us with a seed-picture or concept. In business, we might have the model of a thriving company or entrepreneur. In relationships, we might hold up an example of a successful union. In life, we have personal heroes. But often our traditional ideals of successful living have broken down. Great companies and countries have gone bankrupt, personal heroes have fallen, family structures have become dysfunctional.

Our salvation is found below our feet, above our head, and within every fiber of our being: it is nature. The ways of our Earth offer a solution for humanity that has worked in the past and will work in the future. The principles of nature offer a model of sustainability that can inspire and potentiate us, a model that we can actually follow.

It's obvious that the one dimension of life that is sustainable, that does not deplete, waste, and poison, is the natural environment. Nature knows how to renew, year after year, eon after eon. Nature has an astonishing genius for longevity. Earth's ecology is the quintessential recycler, renewer, and "re" expert. Nature knows energy, how to generate and create life, conserve it, and regenerate it. There is no waste in nature. Every organism does its thing to the fullest, not doubting or procrastinating, not wondering who it is or what it is to do. Birds don't stop themselves from flying with self-critical thoughts.

Nature's eco-principles are the sustain-abilities that we have inherited naturally and know innately. The sustainable life is not about a return to nature, but a return to our *own* nature. Born of the Earth, we are its inheritance. Out of the dust of stars, we have evolved from the genius of the earliest cell to embody the power of the primordial elements, to experience the wisdom of the animals, the cyclical nature of the seasons, the chaos of creation, and the growth of it all. We are an inextricable part of a vast, interconnected unfurling. On this web of life, we have evolved with the essential qualities of all that has preceded us.

The greatest graphic evidence that we share in most of

nature is that when we look at a human DNA molecule alongside the DNA of a palm tree or penguin, it looks virtually the same to the human eye. Look and you will see that we are one with the Earth and all of its inhabitants, each mirroring the other in its core components, and yet manifesting in a myriad of ways. The most shocking fact that we are indivisibly part of all nature is that, of the trillions and trillions of cells that compose us, only ten percent are inherently human. Our body is literally our Earth. And did you know that the mouse has ninety percent of the same twenty thousand genes that humans have? And that this same mouse has a brain structure almost exactly the same as ours?

Some might say that, because we are emotional beings with a vast range of feelings, nature is not relevant to how we should live. Yet, as we learn more about the fauna and flora of this planet, we know that these have feelings as well. Apes have a well-developed sense of empathy. Plants and flowers are sensitive to the intentions of their human caretakers. Nature may not show "happiness," but when the sun comes out and poppies open up, they seem ecstatic to me. We've all seen the joyous wagging of a dog's tail when we come home, the wailing of an elephant upon the death of one of its herd, and the startled leap of a cat when the vacuum cleaner is turned on. I am sure that all life forms have some level of desire, contentment, and fear, though they might be primarily experienced through physical sensation rather than through emotion.

The universal truths of nature's "green wisdom" lead us to abundant sustainability, for nothing in our experience has functioned like nature as a living paragon for perpetual self-growth, health, and continuous evolution of relationships and commerce. The natural wisdom of the environment is not a theory of sustainability, but a fact. It's a real-life, real-time system that works in all ways. Like a commercial enterprise in the production and exchange of goods and services, which is what business is all about, nature has excelled and prospered for untold eons. As a model of relationships, nature is without equal in its web of life of reciprocity and interdependence. We have only to look at the genius of different ecological systems to see how Earth creates community. And as a guide for physical health, nature is the ultimate teacher of longevity, source of energy, and healer.

To be a viable guide in our changing new world, a plan or roadmap must provide a set of principles and tools for transformation. For personal, social and economic growth, nature is the quintessential mentor in the way it adapts and changes. The natural world is the one constant foundation of life-on-the-move that we can consult with assurance time and time again. Nature shows us the way of eternal change.

The modern human tragedy is that we have forgotten our natural roots and become ungrounded by the arrogance of mental hubris and artificial living. But when balmy winds touch our face, the morning light warms our body, and the song

of the trees reach our ears, we realize that nature is calling us to remember—and to re-member ourselves, to make ourselves whole and at one with nature. When we push forward like the spring and go "winter" inwards under cover, nature is showing us that we are no different from her. Throughout every day and night, nature re-calls us. Let there be no question, we reflect her greatness. We are her children.

Nature may be the map and mentor, but for her to help us, we must take action to embody her principles, the basis for all sustain-abilities. We must live "natural." This begins by simply acknowledging that we belong to the Earth as one of its natural offspring.

JAMES WANLESS, Ph.D.

Acknowledging our inherent, undeniable, and inescapable naturalness, we receive the gifts that nature's way of life has bestowed upon us: universal eco-skills for continuously re-energizing and regenerating ourselves.

These eco-principles apply across the board to every person, every relationship, every social institution, and every culture. This ecologic vision is so simple, universal, and natural that anyone at any time and any place can be guided by it.

Who are you?
The window sign
Is everywhere around you.

Looking outside, you see within.
Looking outside, you see why.
Looking outside, you see how.

You are the tree, branch out.
You are the mountain, stand up.
You are the lake, go deep.
You are the rainbow, make magic!

Creation of the Earth,
The Earth is yours
to steward
and create
yourself
again.

Part Two:
THE SUSTAIN-ABILITIES

We've got the map, mentor, and motivation for sustainability; do we have the means? Absolutely. As creatures of nature, we possess the "sustain instinct." We are innately gifted with nature's sustain-abilities, but they have been overridden by our thinking mind. For every one connection between our physical senses and our brain's capacity to interpret the input, the mental brain has ten other connections that run down our bodies to gather the bodily input. Wow! We live in a mental world with a physical, instinctual body, so we have to reprogram and redirect our mental mind to reclaim our sustainability instincts. The sustain-abilities in the upcoming chapters are basically about remembering our natural selves. As Plato once said, "Becoming awake is anamnesis"—in other words, the process of remembering who we've been and where we come from, which is our instinctual existence.

4: Whole and Healthy

One of the most obvious things we can learn from nature is sustainability through wholeness. Nature creates and recreates (sustains) itself because it is one whole system—an eco-community. For me, the most compelling image in history is the picture of Earth from space. We see oneness, one complete sphere. Wholeness is not just a worldview; it is literally *the* world view.

Our lonely planet amid the immense dark is an intricately balanced and interconnected living system, connecting the tiniest cells to the expansive cosmos so that all work together to form a dynamic unity of diversity. Earth is synergistic—each and every part feeding and fueling other parts to continuously energize and re-energize life into one vast, pulsing orb. The precision of how all the different moving parts on Earth coordinate, cooperate, collaborate, communicate, co-create and co-evolve is dazzling and truly miraculous.

From this Earth-view, the ecology of wholeness means that everything is integrated and all parts work together in synergy—a sign of a healthy system, whether it be a human being, the biosphere, any social group, political arrangement, or economic organization. The sustainability of all these living systems, including our selves, must be whole in order to be healthy. Any kind of disconnection or

division compromises and wounds a system, and, without some kind of healing process, renders it unsustainable. As it is often said, "United we stand, divided we fall." This most fundamental sustain-ability takes you to a deeper, more expansive and responsible awareness of yourself. Because how we perceive is how we believe; to live sustainably, we need to think "healthy," about everything. See yourself from the lens of oneness and act in the interest of wholeness. Be inclusive. One for all, and all for one.

Take care of yourself to become completely healthy. We individual selves are a community of inter-dependent parts, an eco-system of different functioning internal intelligences that include the essential four faculties of thinking, feeling, sensing, and knowing. To have a healthy, synergistic, whole self means to balance, integrate, and simultaneously fully engage mind, heart, body, and spirit—to be creative, happy, well and wise. The base sustain-ability is this wholism. We are like trees; if we want to keep standing, we need roots. Like a building, we need a foundation with four cornerstones. Health is not just a physical thing. Far from it; sustainable health is a mix of all our parts functioning well and together. Are you "healthy everything?"

As we know from the basics of ecology, every organism is born to be inter-dependent with the environment in which it dwells. We inhabit many environments with which we need to be synergistic, and this includes our natural world along with all our social environments of family, friends, company, team, community, country, world, and more. There is no way we can sustain ourselves without also sustaining within the many habitats in which we live. These habitats must be healthy if we are to be healthy.

Humanity is replete, however, with disconnections, which do not augur well for us. I see our estrangement from the natural world, and from our own nature as part of the natural world, as a primary source of our physical, psychological, and spiritual dis-eases. We now have a recognized pathology that's called "outdoor deprivation disorder." This is un-whole, unsustainable behavior.

And is our natural environment healthy? In the increasing and disastrous separation of nature and humankind, only respect for and living with nature can restore the balance and secure our sustainment. Earth is not at risk; we are, unless we live by its rules. Remember, nature bats last.

Are our social environments healthy? I am not sure, for we see a world full of divisiveness. To sustain, our world needs to reconcile men and women, young and old, poor and rich, nation and nation, friend and stranger, people and Earth. To change and unite the world, we must change our language, especially from the "either-or" bias to "both-and." The word "and" needs to become the most important concept in our language. I like what Thomas Berry, the great Earth historian and philosopher, wrote in *The Universe Story Book*: "The new prosperity requires a new language. This new language is primarily the language of the Earth, a language of living relationships that extend throughout the universe."

Inclusive synergy is the holistic secret of sustainability, though it's been tried in recent social and economic environments and has encountered difficulty and failure. It's not so easy, and it can take generations for natural ecologies to organize. Synergy is not a quick fix; it's about sustaining—taking time, experimenting, doing it right, thinking long-term, sometimes mistaking, and always remaking.

When things become unhinged, the fine art of wholeness is healing, to make whole. How do we reconnect, reform, and rebuild what has collapsed and been destroyed? To be in sync and synergized implies that every element has empathic knowledge of the others and that they all encounter mutual experience. Thus, to re-sync and re-combine requires the understanding that what's going on outside of us is what's going on inside of us. It's all one.

Self, society, and nature are reflections of each other. Thus, an energy crisis on Earth mirrors our own personal energy depletion. The quest for renewable energies is similarly felt within as we seek to renew ourselves. As I remember to take my grocery bag to the store so that I don't add to the floating plastic continent in the Pacific Ocean, I am reminded to live a cleaner, unpolluted life of greening myself internally. If we want to heal and change the world, we must be the change within ourselves.

This "micro-macro," "inner-outer," "as above-so below" unity is wholeness consciousness. This eco-perspective is a subtle and substantial awareness that leads to a more complete way of being, an integrated life, and enables the all-important, imperative sustain-ability of growth that co-evolves with all that is.

5: Change-able

To sustain in changing times, be changing yourself. Though we are adaptable animals, we resist change. We are still creatures of habit. We look for the easy way in life, and change is work. The forces of entropy take their toll on our motivation and energy to change. Change implies all those imperative but dreaded "re" words—revise, refine, rework, remodel, revamp, reorganize, reorder, rebuild, restart, redesign, restyle, rethink, reinvent.

Somehow, we prefer the devil we know over the unknown and uncertain, regardless of whether or how the new might be better than our current circumstance. We don't trust mystery. We like to think we're in control, and change suggests that we've lost it or are losing it.

In fact, change is renewing and good for the long run. It's taxing and may seem like a setback, but ultimately it's awakening and invigorating. Embrace change as your lifeline for long-term renew-ability and viability. There are different kinds of change requiring different skills, and they all need to be in play for us to keep playing. These change-able skills are adaptation, growth-change, cyclical renewability and recycling, and breakpoint/breakthrough.

Adapting

Adaptive changing is an ever-present necessity for sustainability. That's why we are using the active word *changing*, rather than the static *change*, because each day brings new challenges and new opportunities to be continually adapting. Say "yes" to new ways, and new opportunities will arise. It's an abundant world of new and different, and unless we are actively changing, we fall off the sustainability path, which is a journey that requires constant access to information, monitoring what's going on in a changing world full of surprises, detours, setbacks, openings, re-routings, breakthroughs, and obsolescence. It's no wonder that yoga is so popular, as life today is for the flex-able, the adapt-able, the change-able. Do something different today to support your lifestyle "yoga" of adapting.

Growing

For the long haul, other than day-to-day adapting, subscribe to "growth change." In nature, as long as things are growing, they are regenerating and renewing. So keep growing. This does not necessarily mean growing larger, as in a bigger waistline, house, or business. "More" can be more unsustainable. That's why there's a call for breaking up banks that are too large, too fat, to save. Sustainable growth is gaining a better quality of life, and that means growing yourself—activating and developing latent qualities, sharpening skills, and expanding your inner and outer resources and situations.

We often talk about "building" our lives—building character, building a business, building a body. Building is an old, industrial-age way of development that is engineered, scheduled, and idealized; a construction, fabrication, and artifice, efficient and goal-obsessed. It's not a human model but a mechanical way. Machines break down because of too much repetition, which is unsustainable depletion.

The sustainable way focuses on growing as a way of creating long-term viability and present-time happiness. It is a natural, organic, humane, joyous, and restorative process that is healthy and whole. Grow yourself, grow your relationships, grow your business, grow everything, and live a heartfelt, intuitive way of life that preserves a quality of life and produces ongoing life. That's the new success.

As we grow, the world around us, including relationships, business, and everything else, grows along with us. This is true in nature through co-evolution, in which different natural domains influence the development of one another. The most interesting evidence of co-evolution for me is how plants and flowers were absorbed into Earth's rocks, which led to wondrous gemstones and other mineral forms. So, as we and our world co-grow, new opportunities abound. Look at how new trends in the world are enriching your business and your life.

Growing yourself to sustain yourself is both a dynamic branching out from and digging in to the inner core of who you are. Think of yourself as a tree. This may seem strange, but trees can tell us much about our sustainability. In fact, the oldest living organisms on the planet are the five-thousand-year-old bristlecone pines. Having been among these gnarly creatures, I can tell you that they couldn't care less about what they look like, yet they have a golden vibrance and wild vitality.

Dissemination

Seeds

Seed of Potential

Like trees that grow to their fullest, develop yourself into the full tree that you are meant to be. What does your DNA "seed" say about your natural-born talents? Remember, the nut (seed) doesn't fall far from the family tree. Yet, through the wondrous process of epigenesis, you are changing your old DNA (perhaps by just reading this book). In a way, we can pick and choose what parts of our genetic history we want to keep, to release, and to develop.

Trees grow into the full manifestation of their seed potential because they know absolutely who they are. To be your full self, know yourself. Human growth is a continuing and creative process of figuring out who you are and who you're becoming. Knowing yourself is a lifelong endeavor, so keep seeking yourself. Introspection and self-reflection are a major part of your unfolding. The process of self-exploration is itself a creative flowering. Seeking is its own reward.

Roots of Strength

Keep growing your roots as you dig in, searching for stronger standing in the world, knowing more of your stuff, getting more established, growing a supportive network, and developing a reliable set of lifelines and resources. Are you rooted?

Are you rooted in a sustainable environment? The amazing bristlecone pines have chosen their home in remote mountain heights, which give them clear, fresh air, untouched ground, plenty of bright sunshine, and changing weather. There's so much to be said for living and working in a healthy and creative environment that provides the conditions for viable growth.

Trunk of Repetition

The trunk of the tree of our selves is what we are doing with ourselves, the life we lead that is evident. As we keep circling around, doing life over and over, we experience our own growth rings. We need this kind of normalcy, routine, and focus to sustain. We become habitual creatures as we strive for consistency, efficiency, and ease. How would you identify and describe your focus now?

Branches of Transformation

To really grow, expand, and extend your presence, branch out from your trunk and stretch your limbs. Broaden and diversify yourself by seeking new and different experiences, cultivating various interests, making new friends, saying yes to opportunities, learning skills, traveling, reading, gaining new perspectives about yourself from personal growth workshops. Transform setbacks into advances and disappointments into wisdom. How are you branching out?

Falling Leaves

In the fall season, some trees (deciduous) drop their leaves so that they can endure the sparse, cold winter. Letting go of leaves allows the tree to conserve energy and sustain. We try to be evergreens—on and full all of the time. However, our tendency is to carry on with the same old stuff and baggage and we get fat, stuffed, and immobilized. Periodic downsizing gives us new life. We become leaner and greener. What are you releasing? This can mean dropping beliefs, emotional attachments, old habits and situations—everything from internal issues to external heaviness.

Fruits of Growth

The fruition of our tree-like growth and the highest expression of ourselves—the fulfillment of destiny—is attained and sustained by an ongoing simultaneous turning inward to your core self along with outward extension in the world. By consciously engaging this natural maturation, you get better with age, just as the giant redwoods become more productive, more of everything, as they seem to grow young rather than get old.

What are the fruits of your labor? How are you flowering? What harvest are you reaping? How is your fruition contributing to the living of your destiny?

Slow Growth

Though bristlecone pines live in a remote and somewhat inhospitable terrain, they are uncontaminated and not interfered with; they grow together as a family and community, so they have the elements of sustainability. And they know how to grow slowly. In this world of "now," "fast," "at the speed of blur," it's a change-able skill to know how to "do slow"—slow food, slow eating, slow thinking, and slow growing. The bristlecone pines sustain in a cold environment with dry soil and high winds, which keeps them growing slowly. Growth is not an overnight process; sometimes adversities force us to dawdle along, which could lead us to a healthy and long, quality life. Be patient and persevering.

Bark of Protection

The X factor that the bristlecone pines have is that they know how to protect themselves. Life is full of challenges, competitors, and demons that block and limit you. As with trees, there are a lot of critters (people) out there who would feed on you. We need some kind of protection and preservative. Bristlecone pines have a very thick and robust layer of resin that gives them impenetrability. Learning from these ancient pines, we need thick skin so that we don't take everything so personally, so that the rain flows off our back and we ignore and repel critical barbs. We generate and grow our boundaries from within and without, often becoming so defensive that we bark and turn aggressive, which puts us at risk. What's your protective bark, your protective strategy?

Recycling

Though we seem fixated on a linear view of time, growth and life, in fact, go through cycles. Everything living, including us and all our endeavors and activities, experience the universal cycle of life. Think seasons. Everything, every phenomenon, cycles from the winter time of preparation, planning, and gestation to a spring beginning; to a summer cycle of nurturing, protecting, and maintaining what's been started; to an autumn harvest of completion, fruition, and fulfillment. Which cycle are you in now?

By moving through these inner seasons in all endeavors of life, we are renewed and regenerated. We are recycled and reborn by the cycling process. We experience this cyclical nature of life every day. That's how we can essentially do the same thing day after day. We go from the restoration of rest and sleep (winter), to a fresh morning start (spring), to a work routine (summer), to an evening reward and satisfaction (fall). Through conscious awareness of the dynamic patterning of this life cycle, our days and nights become more meaningful. As energy follows awareness (or are one and the same), the more conscious we are of the cycling of life, the more we are re-energized and re-created by it.

Rejuvenation and sustainability don't just refer to the endless repetition of this daily cycle. They're also about larger life cycles—circling from the beginning spring stages of exploration like a young person dating and beginning a new career; moving on to a summer-like normalization of a stable job, relationship, and home; maturing to fall-like career success, family, and community; then moving into a recycling cycle from family or career to what's next—second spin, second wind, and second life.

Breaking Through at Breakpoint

As is universally true throughout nature, to fulfill the highest potential of our selves, there comes a time for a breakthrough or breakout. The danger is that we get too comfortable with ourselves and are unwilling to recognize that there's a higher state of fulfillment that enables us to live our destiny. These kinds of breakpoints are experienced by people in a midlife opportunity crisis who seek a career or marriage change, by those nearing retirement, or by mothers whose children move out on their own, giving them a chance, perhaps for the first time, at a second life, the freedom and inspiration to discover their own thing.

On occasion, we are forced into big change by a momentous change of circumstances, a great new opportunity, or perhaps a breakup or breakdown. For example, America faces its own breakpoint as it must move from an industrial to a service economy to reclaim its promise as a country. This is a structural challenge, a midlife crisis, that's not just about fixing the monetary or fiscal system, but requires real rejuvenation—breakthrough change!

We all have breakpoints in our lives, the most critical and crucial points on our path. They are not easy, but the following is what you can do to acquire a change-able mentality and proficiency.

Here are some how-to's for breaking through:

- *First, know that these breakpoints will occur. Expect the unexpected. Be prepared by previewing the possibilities of the worst-case and best-case scenarios of your life situations.*
- *Make small changes continuously and progressively to get familiar with changing.*
- *Always see every change as an opportunity!*
- *Constantly prune what you don't need and pare away what doesn't work.*
- *When you make a breakthrough, tell others about your change plans. Have friends, a coach, or a support group to give you encouragement and guidance.*

- *Regularly visualize, feel, and believe your heart-vision of your life destiny and of yourself being successful.*

- *Create yardsticks to get feedback and measure your progress.*

Part Three:

SUSTAINABLE YOU

6: Creative Mind

The formula to sustain yourself is quite simple: Exercise and apply the sustain-abilities of your whole self—creative mind, emotional motivation, physical rejuvenation, and spiritual inspiration—to attain a state of personal synergy that keeps on burning and re-powering.

These are highly creative times, and to sustain yourself, you must live creatively. If you're not creating and re-creating yourself, you are not keeping pace. If you're not creative in the workplace, you fall behind. If you're not creative in relationships, they get old, habitual, oppressive, and dead. To paraphrase the saying, if you're not busy creating, you're busy dying.

Creativity is a sustain-ability initiated mentally, so what can we learn from nature about a creative mind? Our ability to reason separates us from the rest of the sentient world. Nature does offer, however, the essential basics for the creative mind—the fundamentals of mental health that must be adhered to for a flourishing creative life.

Positivity

As I look at nature, it strikes me that that all life forms are positive. Whatever we call their governing intelligence, animals and plants always act in a life-affirming way. They don't get critical, cynical, and depressed like us. They do not poison themselves with life-negating thoughts. Our self-destructive thinking prevents us from being the creative beings we are meant to be. The message is clear: Always be positive minded.

Self-Belief

Another observation of nature is that all organic life believes in itself. Worms, for example, don't doubt themselves. They live the worm life full on. Meanwhile our infamous inner critic betrays us into not believing in ourselves. The power of the mind is so great that we become our thoughts (even though we are not), so if we don't believe in ourselves, then we are not ourselves. We are compromised and flawed, which is unsustainable. There is no reason to disbelieve in yourself. Remember the ecological principle of life: you were born into this world as a human being to be a complete and whole human being. Even if you don't believe in yourself, believe in this principle.

Open and Opportunistic

Nature is an opportunistic intelligence, always seeing and seizing available resources. Nature is hungry for life, and with an open and positive awareness, it sustains. The best example of this is bacteria: early on in Earth's evolving history when oxygen was still a deadly gas, bacteria figured out how to use it as fuel. To bacteria, everything is an opportunity. We are composed of mostly bacteria cells.

Opportunity is grist for the creative mill of the mind. Unfortunately, our judgmental mind closes down opportunity after opportunity. When we judge somebody or something as "bad," we shut down. Resources for the creative life come to us through events, situations, and people, and are mostly unforeseen. Every person, every situation, every moment is an invaluable strand for weaving your life. In this state of attentive non-judgment, you will see that everything is a learning

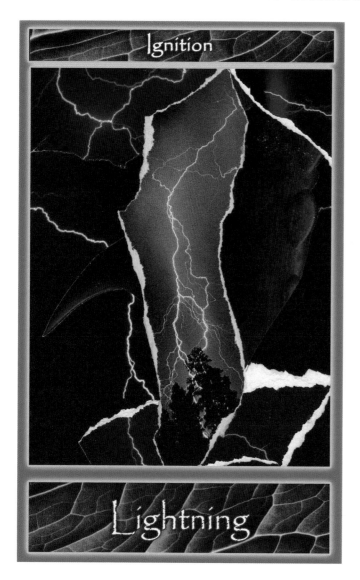

moment, new energy, always of value in some way. Always be open-minded and opportunistic. Say "yes."

Re-Framing

This is where one of those "re"-words is extremely helpful in maintaining positivity, self-belief, openness, and opportunism. For a creatively sustainable life, redefine and re-frame counter-productive beliefs and judgments. If we think of setback as failure, mistake as damning, surprise as a hassle, aging as getting old, being dumped as misery, change as work, then it's true. Actually, setbacks are always opportunities, mistakes are always growthful, surprises are always energizing, aging is always about getting wiser, a breakup is always liberating, and change is always renewing. Always turn negativity into positivity by re-framing your beliefs, perspectives and language.

Intuition

It's remarkable to me how instinctively intelligent nature is. Flowers know when to open, birds know where to migrate, coal knows how to become a diamond, Earth knows how to re-balance itself. Without thinking, nature just knows. It has a built-in logic, an organic way of genius, even to the extent of being mathematically exact. The eons-old mollusk, without a single course in algebra, designed its shell according to the equation of $r=ae$, which the great mathematician, Rene Descartes, discovered just 365 years ago.

From this, we humans can learn to trust our analogue to instinct—that is, intuition. Nature reminds us not to over think. Intuition, which means "tuition or education from within," is direct knowing without rational processes. It appears as an idea, a feeling, a sensation, or a picture in your inner eye that comes out of the blue sky. From the unknown, it just pops up and you just know. Nikos Kazantzakis, author of *Zorba the Greek*, refers to this instinctive, intuitive way of life: "As I watched the seagulls, I thought, 'That's the road to take; find the absolute rhythm and follow it with absolute trust.'"

Moving from *Zorba* to science, we have learned through studies in neuroscience that most of the decisions we make are un-thought and are made in one-quadrillionth of a second (we cannot even begin to comprehend this speed). Either we respond immediately to this intuitive impulse, almost unconsciously, or we don't trust it and spend forever thinking and thinking about what to do. Relying so much on logical left-brain thinking and on our judgmental mind, we doubt the feeling and doubt ourselves, and then we're in trouble. We go into information overload and overwhelm (reacting to "noise" as it's called in communication theory) because of so many possibilities and complexities, resulting in confusion, indecision, and "paralysis through analysis." We know about "survival of the fittest," but perhaps the fittest in today's world are the "quickest!" Procrastination by thinking that obfuscates, muddles, and complicates is an unsustainable trait. "If you wait, get in line."

Ultimately, the intuitive impulse is the decider and ruler of our lives. The quiet revolution going on in psychology today is that it's erroneous to place thinking as the center of our decision-making process. In fact, much deeper, quicker, and subtler intuitions govern us. We waste so much mental power and energy because our thinking brain consumes, in fact, vast amounts of our metabolic energy. We squander so much time thinking instead of following the ABC's of intuition (be Aware of the feeling, Believe it, and have the Courage to follow it).

How to be intuitive? Just let it happen. If you had all sorts of techniques, that would be defeating the purpose. Creative intuition thrives on no rules, no "shoulds," on an empty mind. Because it is such a simple and quick process, we tend to discount it. In modern-day societies, unless something is difficult, time consuming, costly, or comes from an outside authority, it's often not respected. Value what comes up swiftly and easily for you.

There are, however, many caveats and pitfalls about intuition. Do not trust your intuition when you are out of balance—stressed, emotionally upset, overly excited, fatigued, or pressured. Wait until you are centered and composed. Do not trust your immediate intuitions about people, because we are often inaccurate. Intuitions can get us into trouble more often than not because we project what we want to see as the reality. Generally, we see things according to how we are, not about what is. An optimistic person intuits things as good and bright, while a pessimist sees the downside, and both often misjudge the truth about a situation or a person.

Authenticity and Originality

Because we are subjective, irrational, imperfect creatures, our intuition and therefore our assessments and decisions will not always be right; and that's okay, because when we act on our intuitive feelings, we are authentic and energized. True to the impulse that moves us with our own truth, we can be the authors of our lives. Rather than follow somebody else's narrative of how we should live, which is depleting, wasteful, and false, we write our own script for how to live our authenticity. That is what it means to be creative. We are all creative geniuses when we make up our lives our own way. We are a genius version of ourselves, unrepeatable by anyone else. Totally original in our power, we are sustain-able.

Learning

Babies

Learning and Curiosity

The flowering of our authentic, ingenious, creative intelligence is a function of the adventurous mind seeking new learning and experience. Creativity is a mindset that is always open for something new and different, proactively searching for the "wow!" of novelty and stimulus. Creativity is charged by wonder and guided by intuitive hunches that scout and sniff out new trails of possibility. Intuition is a prospecting-like tool that leads you to surprising opportunities and resources. In a sixteen-year study of Nobel Prize winners in the sciences, nine out of ten emphasized that it was intuition that led them to their "aha!" moment of discovery.

Imagination

The magic genie for creativity is imagination. The image we see in our forebrain is an amazing human gift. What we can see, we can be. If you can see it, you know it and can do it. By foreseeing, we can forecast. Imagination is magic! Everything, everyone, every situation is a product of imagination, so the best way to think creatively is to visualize. The power of the picture in your mind's eye informs and catalyzes—as we've all heard, "a picture is worth a thousand words and more." Likewise, Albert Einstein's words, "imagination is more important than knowledge," deserve restating. To live creatively is a far greater sustain-ability than knowing lots of stuff. Unclog the brain of facts and trivia and explore free and open spaces of the imaginal mind for spontaneous insight and original pop-ups.

The red flag about imagination to watch out for, however, is catastrophic thinking: seeing and believing things as much grander or worse than their actual reality. To prevent this kind of delusional thinking, learn to bracket the picture in your mind's eye by seeing the best and worst case scenarios, and then visualizing something in between, which is generally where the truth lies. It is the cognitive bias of the overly optimistic tendency called the "planning fallacy" that leads to false beliefs of over-estimating rewards and under-estimating costs. This is precisely why we took the unwarranted financial risks that brought on the economic depression that began in 2008. Projecting into the future what we see happening in the present often leads to inaccurate—either too positive or too negative—assessments and decisions. Find your state of mental and emotional balance to foresee in a balanced, near-objective way that is on the money.

Whole Brain

Always mindful of utilizing all of our human resources, we need the whole brain to govern ourselves and manifest our creativity. Once we've gotten the "aha!", imagined the possibility, and made the choice or decision, it's up to our left brain to organize and communicate our thoughts. It takes a slow, analytical, and logical mind to put ideas together into a form and narrative that pleases our inherent critical-thinking faculty. We do live in a human world where we communicate primarily by words and sentences that hang together and have a linear logic. It pays to think slow. Even a short book like this one seems to take me forever to write, re-write, and edit, again and again. I call it "smoothing the stone," rounding it into shape so that you can easily get a hold of these ideas.

However, it's because of the tyrannical domination of left-brain logic and judgment in our culture that I was compelled to leave higher academia, and its not-open-enough space for original thinking. Also, what I have learned from life—and not from books—is that the renewable life of creativity is not only mental inventiveness. Innovative living comes from the synergy of the whole brain, which is inclusive of "whole self intelligence"—emotional feelings, the body's sensate wisdom, and the spiritual state of inner knowing and inspiration. Once we've investigated the sustain-abilities of these other dimensions of ourselves, we'll have a more comprehensive understanding of what makes the creative life.

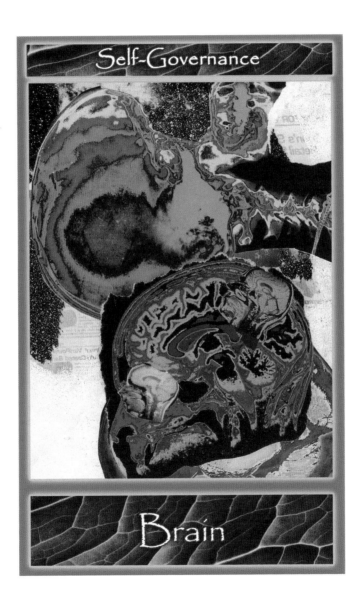

7: Heart of Motivation

On the sustainability trail of wholeness, we now move from head to heart. What can we learn from nature about emotions? Rather than debate what kinds of feelings animals and plants might have, we do know that nature is motivated and enthusiastic about making a living. Being turned on to life is an undeniable, vital sustain-ability.

Fast-forward to where you have achieved some success; perhaps you have built a successful career or business; perhaps you've found your soul mate. You may think you have a beautiful life, but if you are content with it, you are actually at risk. Sustainability and renewability demand motivation and re-motivation. Complacency and comfort are danger signs. To maintain and sustain does not mean to just get along as usual, because change is always afoot; unless you are moved, you tend to resist change, inertia sets in, and the fire of life begins to flicker.

Motivation is emotion put into motion. Our emotions are the motor that get us moving. Emotions are the fuel that keeps us in motion for the life journey. Sustainability is driven by our hearts, the life pump that gets us pumped up. Move to the beat. Movement is life. When you are moved emotionally, you are moved in mind and body.

When you are unmoved and feeling the blahs, try this "emotional fitness" technique. Sound out the blahs and keep amplifying them until you are energized. Or go for a brisk, aerobic walk, breathe in new inspiration and new ideas, and refresh your feelings about life. Remember, heart, body, mind, and spirit are all one interdependent energy system.

We are often ruled by the judge in our head, and we censor and block our feelings. Sustainability is not about being correct in life but being energized by life. Clogged arteries and stuffed stomachs are the result of stuffing our feelings so that we can be proper. It seems like we spend half of our lives denying how we feel. To go along with the crowd of conventionality is a strategy of convenience, but the costs of repression, suppression, and oppression are high. Energy demands release and emotional expression, and damming it all up means we run the risk of living in contradiction and conflict, leading to heaviness and blowups. It's an unnatural act, like damming up the rivers of life.

Emotions animate us and bring us to life. Emotions have intelligence; trust them. How could they not be smart? Engage in heart-stirring for wisdom and innovation. Emotions are inherently expressive. If you can, laugh and cry, wonder and contemplate every day you are alive and well. Fitness means fit to live, and it all starts with the heart of emotion into motion. It's counterproductive and life denying to always be in control. Believe in how you feel and be true to your nature. Be the "weather" that you are, always changing; let it shine, let it rain, and move on.

Heart-Vision

Here's a secret to staying motivated: use your image-making mind in conjunction with your heart of desire. Picture yourself being successful in all areas of life. We all want success. When you see it in your mind's eye, you are moved and impassioned. By repeating this process of picturing the success of

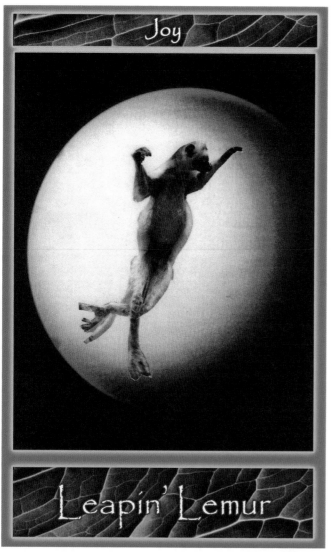

your heart's desire, you can re-motivate yourself again and again. With this continuous and constant motivation, anything is possible. At the very least, you're enlivened, awakened, and rejuvenated. Do this before going to work or when you wake up in the morning to see the wonder of your upcoming day. Have a great day! But visualize it first.

Enjoy the Journey

Live the sustain-ability adage that "the journey is the destination." Enjoy the ride. Isn't this what life is all about? Be grateful and be happy for just being alive and breathing. Have gratitude—it's a powerful sustain-ability—and appreciate all the opportunities, small achievements, and even annoying hassles, because they wake you up and keep you alive.

The emotions of happiness, laughter, and optimism help maintain good health. This is evidenced by a classic Dutch study of ten thousand people over a considerable period of time in which pessimistic, unhappy people were much more prone to disease and earlier death. Optimists are the most sustainable, for they have a stronger immune system, are more psychologically resilient, and live longer on average than their "reality-based" counterparts. In fact, people with broken hearts are far more susceptible to heart attacks. Why do you think that there are forty thousand laughing clubs in India? Those who laugh, last.

For you "brainiacs," keep in mind that joy, fun, and play have been shown to measurably enhance learning and creativity. A happy person is far more receptive to learning, another major sustain-ability.

Because we are so mental and live in our brains, we ignore the actual in-the-moment joy that we feel. Research shows that our memories of something enjoyable are even more enjoyable than the real-time experiencing of it. To fully enjoy the journey, take short time-outs to feel your happy feelings, to breathe in the moment, and savor what your body touches, sees, tastes, hears, and smells. Feel your joy now and express it somehow.

Ride the Waves

I often describe life as an "ocean of emotion." It's full of waves, of ups and downs. Life, at its most basic physical level, is a wave of vibrations. When you have a big decision to make, pick the wave that is your wave; let your heart decide. Since all waves are energy, ride the waves that arise, regardless of whether they are emotions that you enjoy. Every moment and every situation is a new wave of energy, so recognize it and be driven by it. Kowabunga! Surf's up, always. Even when you're down, surf the down. Get off on it so that you can get off of it.

Emotional Intelligence

On a more subdued note, since we are a brain-heart continuum, there are instances when it's wise to mediate certain emotions. Do this by re-framing the difficult ones. Accept and surf the emotional waves, and you will transform them. When you re-frame, you turn emotions like anger into power, fear into excitement, disappointment into acceptance, stagnation into restoration, sorrow into liberation. It's all energy, and how you perceive it determines whether you are a victim or victor of your emotions. We have choice. Follow the energy.

Emotional Balance

One essential to surfing the waves of life is balance. Surfing life is an ever-shifting balancing act. Rather than getting too high or too low and going over the falls, try mindfulness, a meditation technique where you simply observe without judgment how you are feeling and acting. This puts you—naturally, without effort—into a state of equanimity and emotional equilibrium. Ideally, be continuously aware of your feelings and actions; this is like a twenty-four-hour meditation. It's been my experience that this quality of equipoise requires some mindful meditation practice; it's not so easy since we are so full of distractions and judgments. If you can do this, you will be simultaneously in the emotion and also apart from it—on the wave yet not, in the soup yet not. This detachment is your inner balancer that takes you to your center. With a mindful awareness, you are able to release emotions that are not life enhancing, those of avarice, greed, jealousy, resentment, and self-pity. Most eastern spiritual practices, from martial arts to yoga to formal meditation, teach this way of being.

8: The Renewable Body

Nature is active. To renew and re-energize our bodies, we must be physical! The rule of nature is "use it or lose it." So, keep it moving, keep it working. Another rule of nature (and physics) is that a body at rest tends to stay at rest (death) and a body in motion tends to stay in motion (life). You can choose to not sit down and sit on your life. The very latest studies indicate that even wiggling, fidgeting, and squirming about is food for the body, which craves exercise. We are composed of atoms, so keep hopping and bopping, grooving and moving, because that's what atoms do. Live an atomic life, where micro-movements are good and amazingly effective.

It's obvious that mind and body are related. For example, our vaunted critical thinking faculty that depends upon the adversarial and analytical "but" leads directly to procrastination and sitting on our butts. Stop saying "but" all the time to avoid getting out of your chair or off your sofa; to avoid a bigger butt, avoid the seductive, addictive, and unhealthy lifestyle.

Fountain of Youth

Throughout human history, we have looked over and over for the Fountain of Youth. It does exist and you have it right now. It's called exercise. My father, who lived to the age of ninety-nine, was a model of movement. He lawn-bowled until he died. He went for walks. He climbed the stairs of his senior facility. He even had a girlfriend (she was ninety-nine-and-a-half). As for his sex life, I don't know, but we do know that orgasm, according to recent studies, makes you smarter and younger. Again, we are reminded, "use it or lose it," particularly for men who want to stave off prostate cancer.

The Renewable Energy Diet

We all need fuel for the physical journey of our body. So what does nature prescribe? How about clean, renewable energy. It's called the "energy diet," a synergistic blend of the elements: fire, air, water, and Earth. Our focus should be on the elemental energies, not solely on food and drink.

Let's start with the big energizer, the source of life in the sky – Sun! Get outside, get outside, get outside, eat the light. We know that vitamin D is one of the latest and greatest health vitamins that comes best in its natural form—sun and green foods—and even the American Medical Association declared years ago that despite some of the dangers from the sun, an optimally healthy person needs two hours of natural daylight every day. I go to the dermatologist twice a year for various sun-generated skin weirdness, but without regular doses of sun, I am not healthy. I know this is true.

In one study, scientists found that those with the highest vitamin D levels had longer telomeres (the ends of cells that get shorter each time a cell divides), which gives these people five extra years' worth of cell division.

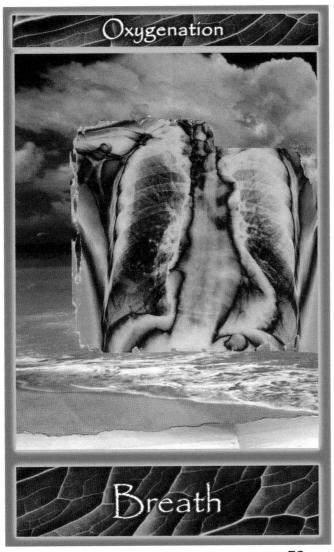

The other great Fountain of Youth and an integral part of the energizer regime is right under your nose—air, or breath. So, inhale life. Neuroscientists have repeatedly shown that aerobic exercise, including simply walking fast and breathing hard a few days a week for half an hour or so, grows new brain cells. Your brain literally becomes younger, years younger than when you first start "breath-walking." This has changed my life.

Strong breathing is vocal; however, for some reason it's not polite to be so audible. If you sound-breathe into a hum or other sounds, high and low, you rev up the body and activate your trillions of cells, which love you for that. As my expression

Sustenance

Water

coach, Wowza, says, "Move your vowels every day." Silly, maybe; but energizing, absolutely. It's the sonic tonic. Tone yourself with your tones and tunes. For a sound body, sound out.

What about water? Well, we know that nature does not drink processed liquids, diet drinks, caffeine, or alcohol. Talk about self-pollution. Like nature, drink god-juice—clean, natural water. And drink enough. I had the mysterious "chronic fatigue syndrome" years ago and the combination of being nice to myself and drinking water cured me. I was dehydrated. The next time you are not feeling well, water, water, water. Go to the well to get well. It circulates and purifies your precious bodily fluids.

Here are some factoids about water: Do you know that one fifth of the world's population does not have access to clean, drinkable water? No wonder there's a health crisis. Do you know that a week's exposure to the sun in a glass bottle will purify the most contaminated water?

Now, for the Earth element. Eat real food. Eat less food. Eat better food. Eat local food. Eat diverse food. And don't eat sugar, don't eat late, don't eat fast. One of my favorite Earth foods is soil. Not that I eat it, but it's absolutely astonishing to know how many nutrients and billions of helpful bacteria enter your body when you stick your hands into the soil. The same occurs when you go barefoot in the park. It's so saddening to see people avoiding contact with nature against their bare skin, hands, or feet, when immersion in nature is the healing rejuvenator. From mud baths to hot springs to walks in the woods to jumping into the sea, soil and water make up the energy diet for living well and living long.

The Ultimate Regenerator

Sleep. Without it, we are crazed, cranky, and dull. We all know the right and wrong things to do for a good sleep, but nevertheless, for many it's the most vexing thing. I know; I travel a lot. What has helped me more than anything, as I go through many time zones—from Asia to California to New York to Holland in a span of two weeks of work— is "bed meditation." It sounds strange, but when my body wakes up at three a.m. ready to go, thinking it's somewhere else, my brain takes a few moments to remember where I am. While it does this, I just lie there and do the Vipassana technique of feeling my body, going up and down from head to toe and back again. Amidst this, I have worrisome thoughts—the upcoming workday, not enough money, the wrong things I've said, emails I need to send, sinus congestion, unpressed shirts, on and on—yet I keep going back to scanning and feeling my

Sleep

Bear

body without judgment, even my aching head. Awareness is energy, so when we focus on something like our bodies in a meditative way, we energize ourselves while simultaneously calming it. Meditative yogis hardly sleep. So, although I may not sleep many hours in a night, after this nocturnal meditation, I feel good, and my energy is up. I'm okay. It's astonishing, really. Sleep must be right up there with our highest priorities for the sustainable life.

Neoteny

Sustainability is not just about longevity. What's the point of living long if you are sick and in pain? Sustainability focuses on the "health-span," not so much the life-span. Aging well is a sustain-ability, and a major contributing factor to this is having "attitude." Those cultures in which people live long and well are not the result of their magical water, their diet, or their air. It's a mental attitude of neoteny—growing young—by maintaining child-like behavior: playfulness, physicality, playmates, adventure, spontaneity, exploration, emotional expression, creativity, even foolishness. Death by seriousness stalks everyone. Adulthood can be adulterating—contaminating the fountain of youth. As adults, we assume we should be responsible, parental, lead and control our lives. Who is in control, anyway? Not us, but the all-mighty universe in which we are but a speck of a speck of a speck. Like a child who trusts its parents, we "adults" need to trust our parents—our DNA, our sun, which we assume will be around tomorrow, our instinctive intuitive intelligence, and the life-force that gave us life. Let go, let god, have fun—live healthy and long.

9: Inspired Life of Destiny

The inspired life: what does that mean, and how does it help us sustain? Inspiration is a concept that means "inspirited," or infused with something extra-special like a calling from the divine, or a consuming passion. Different from motivation, which is short-term desire, inspiration is a long-term dedication to some kind of transcendent cause or overarching vision or dream you have for yourself. It's your destiny.

We all have a destiny, and once you get it, you are inspirited because you have the greatest ally, the life-force on your side, which gives life and sustains life—whether we call it the Great Spirit, universe, god/goddess, Source, the Creator.

Amazingly and obviously, nature gives us the secret for discovering this inspired way of life. Observation of nature shows us that all life forms know who and what they are and how to live to fulfill their potential, which is their destiny. A rosebush knows it's a rosebush and does its best to be the best rosebush it can be. See how a bird knows how to be a bird, and goes about its business. It does not try to be something it is not. It has no confusion as to which berry to seek. No doubts, no hesitation, no self-questioning. All elements and creatures of nature know themselves, how to actualize themselves and their destiny. If they don't do what they are meant to, they die.

We humans can survive even if we don't do what we're supposed to, but we are broken, in a way. In the mechanical world, if a machine doesn't do what it's meant to, it's broken. Sustainability can be about fixing what's not working. To find your destiny is to become whole and healed—fixed.

The message from Mother Nature is live your destiny, which is a mysterious and miraculous phenomenon. Your destiny is encoded in the essence of you, which has been seeded in your DNA and in your unique body, talents, skills, and personality. Knowing your destiny re-kindles the spark of creation in you into a flame of inspired living that is ceaselessly creative, energized, and committed.

Ignited by inspiration, you are pulled along by this life-force, and you cannot help but accept its future. Once you know who you are meant to be, what you are supposed to do on this Earth, and are naturally swept along to this destiny, there are tremendous benefits, all of which are highly sustainable traits. You can release stress and anxiety, let go of confusion and indecision, be optimistic and positive, motivated from day to day, and energized by living as your authentic self. All of this gives you enormous personal power and effectiveness in the world. And all events, including setbacks and disappointments, are part of the journey and are accepted as lessons, resources, and energy. You don't have to try so hard. You can open up and not be overly competitive and protective of your personal ego. You can enjoy the journey. What's not to like about that?

Why don't we all seek this magical way of life? Because we don't grow up knowing a story of life that includes "know yourself, live your destiny." Rather than find our authentic being, we've been taught to fit into society and live the conventional "good life."

How do we find our destiny, and how do we know it? We can go to a bookstore and look at the numerous works for discovering our life purpose. These books often make the search for meaning a heady project. Once again, back to our nature as nature, keep it simple, and don't over-think. Ask your heart, "What do I desire as my highest expression?" Trust your feelings and emotional intelligence to inform you.

To affirm your inspiration as genuine, visualize in your inner mind's eye a picture of yourself successfully living this aspiration. Using this "heart-vision" as your life destination, choose this goal with intention and set sail. Let your destined future sweep you along with its favorable wind.

You have to believe. If you have any doubts that your aspiration is real and true, you don't have it. Inspired, destined living is not questionable. It's not a mental thought, it's a certainty.

You have to take action. Just because you know your destiny does not mean it's just going to happen. It takes doing, but it makes the doing easier, more fulfilling, more renewable.

You must see some results. I've known delusional people who seem to see and feel their destiny and even take some action believing it's true, but all the evidence belies their thinking. Without some results verifying that you're on the right track, you are only a dreamer.

Intuition is particularly adept at letting you know if you are on your desired course as it constantly updates the state of yourself—your own inner GPS. Intuition is a change-able, current, and evolving source of continuous information and feedback as it directs and redirects you on your path.

It may take years of maturation, experience, growth, and change to find your inspired way. Keep on the search, for it is truly the holy grail of life. Your destiny is a cup that endlessly fills you with energy and motivation—an elixir that heals you, the ultimate energy drink that propels you.

There is no guarantee, however, that you will realize your apotheosis of highest self-expression and totally manifest your destiny according to how it's exactly imagined. Unforeseen things happen, mystery rules. Inspired living, though, gives you the greatest possibility for sustaining a fulfilling, successful life. That's the most we can ask for: the chance.

Like everything in life, things change and we change. Always check in while on your voyage of destiny, riding the magic carpet of your imagination that transports you. I've always felt that I was on my authentic path, yet was never truly destiny-inspired. However, we do evolve. We are a process of endless unfolding. As Michelangelo once said about making his sculptures, "I see the angel in the stone, and I chisel and chisel until she is set free." It takes a lot of chiseling, getting rid of what we are not, or thought we should be, or of what's become old and redundant, until we reach deep into the original seed of potential that we are supposed to become.

Complex creatures that we are, our destiny may be a series of seasons and seasoning where we continually re-feel, re-define, and re-imagine ourselves. At least once a year, during an "inner winter" introspective time, re-view your heart-vision. Without an emotionally charged vision of ourselves, we are rudderless and without sail on the sea of life.

It wasn't until very recently that I really felt and saw my apotheosis. Through a convergence of circumstances and good fortune where preparation meets opportunity, I got my inspiration, my mojo, and my destined path. This book, in fact, is a manifestation of that revelation.

10: Synergy!

As we see a mad scramble by countries for energy sources in the world today, we also search for more energy within ourselves. Energy is precious, and the bottom, bottom line of sustainable success. The survivors and winners in life are those with the most energy. With energy, anything is possible. Without energy, nothing happens.

The common denominator of all the personal sustain-ability centers we've discussed already is their energizing effect. Intuition is an energy-impulse, subtle, but always a stimulus. Emotions move us into action. The renewable body is energy in motion. The inspired life pulls, pushes, and grows us.

When these different energy sources work together, the result is synergy, an exponential increase of energy where the whole is greater than the sum of the parts. This is how the Earth, the sun and the universe sustain—through the continuous synergy of an interconnected energy system.

Synergy is ever-renewing and re-energizing. Each of our personal sustain-abilities is a center that energizes the others, thus creating a continuous personal powerhouse. Without all these centers turned on and active, we burn out; have no back-up or pick-up, not enough juice. One could have the greatest body in the world or be a mental genius, but if these gifts are not supported by the emotions of joy and spiritual purpose, they are limited and ultimately unsustainable because they are not renewable by the whole self. If, for example, you want to do something but your body is not physically up for it, you create little. Perhaps your spirit is willing to take on an endeavor, but you don't believe in it and so little is manifested. Maybe something seems like a good and practical idea, but it doesn't have bite, doesn't grab you and turn you on; not much happens.

Creative Manifestation

Synergized, we become a veritable sun of ever-creative expansive energy. (The word *synergy* originates from *sun ergos*—sun energy or synergy.) Like the synergistic sun, our own wholeness is a potentiated, exponential expression of ourselves.

Energy is power, and power manifests something new. We often think of creativity as some kind of special mental skill or genius, when it's really whole-self energy (our inner energy, or "innergy") that has been unleashed in unison. Energy in motion is inherently creative, always changing the status quo. Create energy to manifest.

Think about it. When you want to make something happen in your life, all the basic centers of consciousness and energy must function as one. When you desire something, your emotions are engaged. When you have an idea about how to do it, a belief that you can, a picture in your mind's eye of seeing yourself do it, your mental mind is fully utilized. You then take some action because your physical body has been mobilized by your turned-on heart and head. You have then manifested something and your life-force spirit, source of creation, has been tapped and expressed.

Life Navigation

When you make decisions to navigate a sustainable life, follow the energy of your whole self. Ask how your heart feels about it, what your mind thinks, what the body senses, and what your wise spirit knows. When they are all aligned, you have an empowered, unanimous decision. You are creating synergy, and that will take you places.

Do a synergy inventory by asking yourself whether all the power centers in you—mind, heart, body, spirit—are in harmony with what you are doing for work, who you relate to, and how you are living. This examination is not only about your basic state of healthy wholeness, it's about your personal power, which is your energy and how you channel energy to live your destiny, make things happen, and receive what you most desire.

Energize by Expression

Energy must have a release for it to be potentiated. It needs to be actively expressed. Blocked energy creates introversion, depression, and ill health. All healthy life circulates, taking in and putting out like breathing. For realizing your potential and power, your energies need to be expressed by a life full of friends and loved ones, by making a productive living, and establishing a home base and community. These life necessities are sustainable when they are synergistically expressed with your energy centers.

When you are not synergized within yourself and with your work, home, and relationships, the result is "unergy"—the exponential decrease of power. Your life becomes depleted, wasteful, and probably toxic. Not good. In nature, everything is in ecological harmony and synergistic. A tropical fish is not found in cold water. The right sustainable situation does not mean just comfortable and stable; it must be synergistic and energizing!

Attraction

Each of us is a veritable force field of energy. We transmit and we receive. Dynamic and

magnetizing, we not only create, we attract. We bring in what we put out, so the greater our expressive energy, the more we draw to us—more opportunities, resources, sustenance, and energy. Again, it is our synergy that magnifies our power of attraction, so it takes not just the requisite intention through invocation and affirmation, but also great desire, self-belief, physical health and stamina, spiritual vitality, purpose, and action, action, action.

Conservation

We've talked about creating and renewing energy; how about conserving it? Somewhat paradoxically, the best way to conserve is to create. Preservation by creation. Again, use it or lose it. But if we act willy-nilly on this and that without whole-self agreement and inner self energy consensus, "unergy" results.

Sometimes we just need to say "no," not in a negative sense, but rather in the positive use of the word, which is saying "yes" to something else. Say yes to yourself, to your energy, your truth, your heart, your body, your destiny, your future, and you will naturally conserve and perpetuate yourself. This requires your sustain-ability to say "no" to waste, depletion, toxicity, and "yes" to boundaries, self-integrity, healthy limitations, and long-term future.

Conservation is, of course, an eco-principle of recycling and renewing through the inner seasons, particularly the sustain-ability of "wintering" yourself—stopping, cocooning, sleeping, resting, meditating. And be nice to yourself by going to your sources of regeneration: a book, a massage, a movie, a walk, a bath.

Part Four:

SUSTAINABLE WORK

It's clear that if you don't produce in the business of living, you are not sustainable. We know from nature that all of life is fully engaged in its work and does so with total sincerity and gusto. We are meant to be productive and active in the world, creating services or goods to exchange with others so that we can all live. There is no greater waste than not fully using your skill set in the world. It's a waste of human resources, and a social waste, when we do not contribute to our community through our work.

11: Productive Right Livelihood

What we can learn from nature about work is that all of nature knows who and what it is, and does its thing. All fauna and flora produce according to their unique purpose. How do we know what we are purposed to do?

You can read a book on finding your life purpose, you can take a career aptitude test, you can see what kind of work is available, you can check out which jobs pay the most or are the easiest, but you can find your purposed livelihood by asking what your heart would love to do. What turns you on the most? Where there is passion, there is genius and there is success. Ask not what's practical, but what you love. Khalil Gibran wrote that "work is meant to be love made visible." So, do what you love and love what you do, and you will find your niche. This will lead to greater productivity, the realization of your potential, manifestation of your tremendous contribution to the world, and bring you lots of fun! And you can keep going and going.

The most productive people are those who have a renewable work life, meaning that their work works for them and they work for it. Ask yourself, "Does my work energize me and do I energize it?" Does your workplace create you and do you create it? Does your job or career renew you and do you renew it?

In nature, we know this as "mutual symbiosis," which is the most common and usual way that nature functions. To take from the job and only put in your hours, and for the job to take from you—your dignity, your health, your potential, and your growth—is a kind of parasitism, like a "vampire economy," or a win-loss model. Though this predatory style of survival has a role in evolution, symbiotic win-win has a far better chance for evolving and sustaining. Teams of synergy and cooperation succeed and live on.

By having such a symbiosis between you and your work, you are on the path to right livelihood—your profession, place and profits are, at once, your growth path and life purpose, and your passion and play. This high concept is an evolved way of synergistic working and it's the most sustainable because it simultaneously fulfills and energizes you spiritually, emotionally, mentally, physically, and practically in the world. You will be at your most productive.

My own decision to leave a professorial university career in political science for life as an independent spiritual counselor was a bold, intuitive move that fit the criteria for right livelihood. My heart soars when I work and the idea of retirement is like death. This work grows me and I contribute to the field; it feels like what I am supposed to do.

We have it very wrong when we ask what a job can bring us in terms of monetary remuneration, unless of course you really love money. If so, go for it! If you want the best kind of work for sustainability, don't ask what kind of work seems the most stable; look for right livelihood. Instead of just padding your bank account, ask what work fills up your energy bank. Unless money gives you the incentive and freedom to tap your creative potential and life destiny, it can be worrisome and weighty.

Future of Work

One of the most critical sustain-abilities in business is the ability to see ahead to stay ahead. Keep informed. Use your "wisdom nose," as Rumi said, to sniff out what's hot and what's not. Gather intelligence. When ants meet other ants coming from another direction and sniff, they are doing more than just greeting; they are smelling what's ahead. Why are monkeys so endurable? Because they take to the trees to see who's coming. Seals pop their heads out of the ocean to see what's coming down the beach. Information is gold.

I sense that in the future, as we subscribe to sustainable living, we will follow what nature teaches us about the wisdom of the "economics of enough"—do not take more swag than what you really need. Enough is enough. In the future, "more" will mean more energy, not more stuff that becomes baggage and clutter. The new consumption will be less things and more creation. That's food for thought and thought for food. Joy, experiences, people, service, meaning, growth and, of course, enough money are what nourish and fulfill us, not just another gadget and more square footage.

Of course, there is no crystal ball that tells us with accuracy what's going to happen. I call that "prediction fiction." Nevertheless, we all want to know the future, as evidenced by the European Union's staggering investment of one billion euros on a super software program, the Living Earth Simulator, that promises to foretell everything. Really? There are just so many variables, too many surprises like un-computable appearances from nowhere such as "black swans," along with, of course, plenty of "chaos" where a butterfly in Australia can impact the rest of the world ("the butterfly effect"). And as the Heisenberg Principle of physics states, predictions themselves change the future (it's like a coyote trying to bite its own tail).

The best way to predict the future is to create it, so do what you can to innovate your way in your niche. The future belongs to those who create it, yet we still won't know what's going to actually and ultimately happen. Until it happens, by taking proactive, creative steps, more good things happen, and even when things don't go as planned, we are better able to devise a Plan B. Unforeseen opportunities and resources abound and arise.

Solo Entrepreneur

The solo entrepreneur, termed the "solopreneur," is a new version of capitalism, and will hopefully become more evident in the future workplace. Right livelihood is its foundation. It extols individual genius, freedom, and the opportunity for creative and inspired individuals to be well-rewarded in the workplace. Human capital is increasingly cherished and sought after; the eminent management theorist, Peter Drucker, described the future as belonging to the "knowledge worker," whose brainpower is "the most important productive asset of modern society." Those who do right livelihood, which is a whole-self extension of the knowledge worker, are sustainable-rich.

For the right livelihood person, work becomes a vehicle for self-actualization—the realization of potentials and life purpose. This converges with the trend that everyone in the service and information industry, and in the bourgeoning small- and micro-business market, will be their own individual company. It's termed "YouBiz"—you are the business, producing yourself and your skills as an independent, consultant-like entrepreneur responsible for knowing your niche, your stuff, selling, marketing, and branding yourself, innovating, and keeping up.

Collaboration and Communication

In the new workplace, the sustain-ability to collaborate and co-create with shifting teams of people is paramount. The lifeblood of the twenty-first century is communication, because partnering, networking, and teaming have grown exponentially in the relationship world of ours. As always, the business of living is about people and the ability to get along and work along; never before have we experienced this variety, complexity, and volume of interactions. We now engage, on average, 170 interactions in the daily workplace. Wow.

Empathy

The revolution in our collaborative work relationships is how we conduct them. The old style of corporate and organizational bureaucracy is being replaced by a more consensus-based mode. Critical, aloof, analytical, and ego-centered ways of communicating are giving way to more teamwork, openness, respect, and support. This new communication rests on the empathic ability to feel what another is feeling. It's not talking at, but feeling with. That's why we have two ears and only one mouth—so that we listen and listen again before we speak. And it's why we have two feet and only one head: so that we can follow in the footsteps of others and walk their paths before we think and judge. Intuition, this feeling way of knowing, is the magic that entrains and harmonizes us.

The Sustainable Company

If you have a business with employees, and you want a sustainable business, hire and grow sustain-able workers. Have them be solopreneurs in their own right, for they will be self-led and take initiative, all under a common, motivating heart-vision that pictures the collective destiny of the business. Make it your right livelihood, and communicate with your people. Use your natural, intuitive, creative mind; it's given you the creative edge, and it doesn't cost money. Organize your business as a symbiotic team. Keep on changing, adapting, and growing as you grow yourself. Change your routine, do something different and "re," "re," "re."

It's not so much about building a business as it is growing the business. With nature and an organic model in mind, the new leader of a sustain-able business is a gardener. Seed, cultivate, and protect. Be patient and think long-term. Start small and expand only when you have to. Don't be afraid to prune back. It's about quality and not quantity. Tend to the well-being and health of yourself and your employees. Happy plants produce. Happy people are productive.

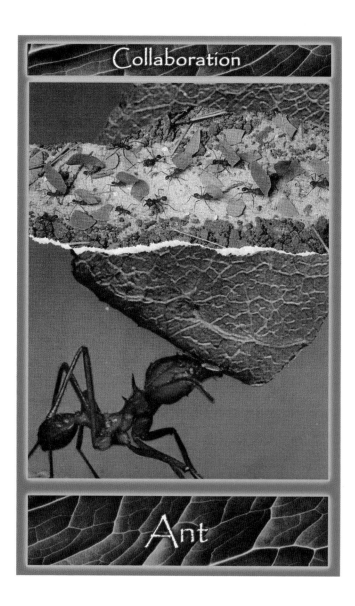

Part Five:

SUSTAINABLE LOVE

Of all the sustain-abilities, love is the greatest sustainer. The will to live and sustain ourselves is rooted in love—love for life—to engage life, enjoy life, endure its many inconveniences, disappointments, losses, and sorrows, and yet desire more life.

Most interpret love as romantic love, but this is only one kind of love. By recognizing other qualities of love in our lives, we are motivated to keep going and get prepared for the rewarding and most complex and evolved of relationships: the love partnership.

Love for life is inclusive. Love yourself. Love others. Love people. Love your work, your home, your Earth. Love is a deep wellspring of sustainability. Even in your darkest moments of despair and discouragement, there's always someone or something to love and be loved by. This force is life-saving and life-giving.

12: Connect, Communicate, Care

Lest we forget, we are social creatures. We are here to commune, communicate, and actively care for each other. The core of our social life is what the Greeks called *agape*: unconditional love for all beings. Reverence for life is a spiritual and perhaps instinctual love that is the underlying, primordial drive that gives us life and is the social glue that bonds us. This is why in every study of longevity that I have ever read, having friends is the single most important factor for a long and happy life—more essential than exercise, positive thinking, eating well, medical care, wealth, and having interests.

The latest research shows that women live longer than men because they are more optimistic about life, and that's because, it is surmised, women have a rich, supportive circle of friends. Men are not as skilled at friendships; they die earlier, and alone. I was always struck by Deborah Tannen's studies of male and female communication styles that indicate women communicate to communicate, while men communicate to get something or to gain relative power. It's a simple and essential fact of life that we need to connect to connect, whether in person, by phone, or on Facebook.

At a dinner party, I was conversing with someone I had never met before when she suddenly said, "I don't know you, but I love you," and slipped a bead bracelet onto my wrist that spelled out, "I don't know you, but I love you." Now, that is agape love (and a skilled way of making a friend). Re-source this feeling within you, because it's the life-sustainer supreme. When we realize and activate this simple and basic life-force, we've tapped into the endless life-spring.

Connection Love

The sustainability message is clear: love, relate to, and engage others, and in a variety of ways, from the basic "hello" to the intimate love partnership. To create and maintain a loving and long life, connect, connect, connect. Unlike in the past, we are now proactive and make new friends, take the initiative, go to meet-ups, network, join an activity, reach out online. Friend is now a verb - "to friend." In the old days, we had automatic friends through a stable family structure, a steady job of work relationships over time, childhood friends from school, and hometown buddies. Now, family as we knew it is disappearing, we move from job to job, and as mobile people with lifestyle choices, we don't often live where we grew up. We become different. We are not homogeneous anymore. Malls have replaced townships. No wonder we "Twitter."

"Liking" and "friending" people are primordial, visceral human needs as basic as eating and exercising, and there's nothing quite like in-person connection. Hearing a friendly voice, shaking a hand, hugging, looking another in the eye, and just feeling their presence makes us feel good and come alive. And it's true that our physical heart responds healthfully to heartfelt connections. It's so amazing to see young people, even kids, texting each other while they're dancing together or in the same room.

In the lonely crowd of our twenty-first century diaspora, pets often satisfy our touchy-feely needs, and more. "Biophilia"—love for all life of all forms—is a proven way of feeling more loving and whole by connecting with nature.

I've seen with my own eyes at my dad's senior care center how the elderly and disabled light up when a service dog enters the lobby. As I stroke the keys on my laptop at this very moment, I am stroking my cat, Jasmine, and the keyboard seems to purr. As kids, who among us didn't love our pets? An Australian study on the healing power of dogs found that the owners of dogs and other pets had lower cholesterol, blood pressure, and heart-attack risk compared with people who don't have pets.

Make "I don't know you, but I love you" a daily sustainability practice. Connect to connect—greet a passer-by with a smile, make small talk and compliment, wave to a person who did you a favor on the road, woof with your neighbor's dog, rub your hands on a tree, feast your eyes on a beautiful flower.

Self Love

It's hard to sustain our lives when we don't feel good about ourselves or appreciate ourselves, let alone like or love ourselves. If we don't value and esteem our self, what's the point of living? This is not a narcissistic thing, not an ego-arrogant, self-adoring thing, but an agape quality of self-reverence for the light and soul that you are. Tell your inner critic to take a hike. Transcend your mental mind. Place your hand on your chest and feel your heart. This will get you in touch with the beauty, sweet fragility, and miracle of wonder that you are.

We all want love, for it's the life-force, the magic potion that awakens our heart. The quickest way to have love that sustains is to love yourself. Take time out for yourself, look at yourself in the mirror, speak to yourself with an affirmation or love poem, or do something warm and nice for yourself—get a massage, take a bath, get a facial, relax in a sauna or a hot tub.

Here's my latest love-verse to myself. It's pretty corny, but love is not about smartness. It's about being open, vulnerable, and pure of sentiment. For most guys this is almost taboo—it's just too silly—but it takes the sustain-ability qualities of courage, self-assurance, and inner strength to reveal your sweetness.

> *I might look old*
> *I am gold*
> *I might forget things*
> *I am bada bing*
> *I might not be perfect*
> *So?*
> *I am*
> *That's enough*
> *For me to love.*

The surest way to love and be loved by another is to love yourself. There is no way you can truly love another without loving yourself. How you relate to another is how you treat yourself. If you're hard on yourself and critical of yourself, it's guaranteed that you will be the same with others. How we see another is how we see ourselves. Perceptions of others tend to be mirror projections of ourselves, or projections of how we would like them to be.

And, of course, what we don't like in another is what we don't like about ourselves. Use this mirror-like feedback and information to compassionately process through your mental judgments to become more open and accepting of yourself and others.

Relationships are our foremost growing grounds, perhaps the most difficult and most effective forum for evolving ourselves into a more whole, clear, and loving person, of ourselves and others. It is through relationships that we confront the shadow side of ourselves and learn to work through and transcend our insecurity, jealousy, judgmentalism, impatience, selfishness, unmindful reactions, blaming, inability to let go, control, and taking things too personally.

So, to become more loving of yourself, grow yourself. It's amazing how much better you like yourself when you work on overcoming weaknesses and blind spots, when you do and learn new things, branch out, and get creative. This good feeling about yourself naturally translates to how you feel about others and how they feel about you. Love attracts love.

Paradoxically, one of the greatest self-loving acts is to give to another, which makes evolutionary sense for survival and sustainability. Acts of generosity make your brain light up and make you happy, according to neuroscience research. We become far more turned on to life and ourselves when we give rather than receive. Help another and help yourself.

Always remember, we are not perfect, and nobody else is either. We are each a work in progress. To me, perfectionism is a social disease, a pollutant under the guise of goodness. Give it up, and just love.

"MYSELF"
I know you
and I still love you.

Inter-Dependent Love

Looking at ecosystems in nature, different elements and creatures probably don't actually care much for each other, but they do value one another. On an instinctive level, animals and plants know to let others do their thing, simply to create a sustainable eco-system—a group of diverse beings that work together for their mutual survival. Plainly put, we need each other. I don't know you, but I love you, and I need you.

Nature is not the dog-eat-dog fiction that some believe, but a far more collaborative and symbiotic community. The evolutionary winners of life, those who survive and sustain, are cooperative teams, not parasitic-like individuals who feed on others. Although ants are mighty warriors with unending, epic, and deadly battles over resources, humans are the only life form that kills others for the sake of killing. We murder our own for an idea, an ideology. From nature's perspective, that strikes me as unergy, un-evolved, and unsustainable.

Nature shows us that groups are sustainable when there's an "eco-nomic ethos", all members subscribing to a win-win model where all benefit. Though we each have our own aspirations, the fundamental value of working together to stay together must prevail for our shared survival. It's actually the most selfish yet the wisest thing to contribute and work for the welfare of all.

Competition, which abounds in nature, is a win-win testing ground for becoming stronger. As much as I dislike conflict and confrontation, it exists, so we must embrace it and compete. Love your "noble adversary," and if they are not noble, "befriend the bastard." It makes us more resourceful, more motivated, more aware, more adaptive—all essential qualities for sustainable living. There is evolutionary wisdom in insecurity, for if this anxiety is not over the top, it does grow brain cells and make us smarter. Welcome the natural system of conflict/cooperation, though it's a messy and delicate ongoing balancing and rebalancing of power.

Belonging Love

To manage and mitigate the destructiveness of win-lose dysfunctional behavior, there needs to be a shared emotional feeling of community. I learned this very clearly in researching my doctoral dissertation, *Keeping Peace Among the Families of the Cosa Nostra* (Mafia). Though there was great greed and tremendous illicit financial opportunities, whatever peace prevailed between the various family gangs was primarily because of their allegiance to their common Italian heritage. They had a feeling of belonging. It was their *cosa nostra* ("our thing").

It's our instinctual nature to desire a sense of belonging and to have emotional loyalty and respect for others with whom we identify. Without any affective connection, we are alienated and isolated. As a result, we as individuals are not completely whole, and a society of estranged members is similarly fragmented and un-whole.

With few exceptions, our traditional "belong-groups"—family, town, church, country—have changed. It's a sustain-ability challenge and opportunity to find substitute fidelities, which we now see emerging in new versions of family and community that have been cobbled and morphed into hybrid "circles of belonging." What allegiance(s) do you feel? If there are no strong sentiments of loyalty to a group, it's a sustain-ability to find or create belongingness.

Family Love

In the old days, our primary relationships of belonging were family. Though family bonds are meant to be deep-rooted and everlasting, that's not so true in the modern world. Because of social and economic upheaval, generation gaps, and change of consciousness, traditional family ties, if they even exist, are frequently toxic and dysfunctional.

But it's a vital sustain-ability to have some sense of family, whether it is your family of origin, your family of choice, your friends, your tribe, your circle of belonging. These evolving forms of the "new family" are our support systems where we can hang out and be heard out. Face-time and real-time friends are the new family of kindred spirits that band together where emotions can be expressed and processed. When sorrow, fears and angers are voiced and vented, we are purified and liberated, which is why support groups of all kinds are so necessary and so popular. We are enlivened and energized by sharing our joys and excitements.

In this "-philia" brand of love, we do things together and have fun. Like a pod of dolphins swimming together, affectionately and playfully create adventures and events that keep our inner child active and enthused. This is particularly important for those who don't have children. Magic happens on a hike, in a cafe, on a road trip, at a birthday. Give heaps of love to your intrepid instigators of these delightful and divine activities.

Unlike "frenemies," the new family circles and tribal pods are composed of genuine life-allies whom you can count on and who have your back. Unconditional loyalty, acceptance, and support are absolutely essential for healthy being. This engenders trust, which is the backbone of every relationship. Without a trusting environment for learning how to trust and become trustworthy, every kind of relationship will encounter the usual saboteurs of suspicion, insecurity, and withholding.

For those with a healthy traditional family—kids, parents, siblings, relatives— count your blessings; you are fortunate. Show up for your reunions. It feels good and right. And it's a karma kind of thing. There are billions of people on the planet, there are millions of years you could have been born and an entire Earth to live on, but you are related to this small family group at this time in history at this place on Earth. There's obviously some kind of connection, and it's got to be respected, valued, sustained, and fulfilled, even though we may not understand it. It's just too amazing to ignore. So, ask yourself, "Why was I born into this family? What am I to experience, complete, and grow?" These questions about your lineage reveal so much about you. Your family is your mirror. Look and learn.

For those who have been dealt a bad family hand, live your truth, say your truth, endure the family until you can't, and then get out. It's probably your karma to learn how to say "no" to your relations and say "yes" to yourself. Through our

experiences, we become stronger. Forgive them and love them, for they have been a stepping stone on the path of your destiny. Just don't step on them—have compassion and be thankful. Move on without guilt from your family of origin, and find a new family of choice.

Teamwork Love

Beyond the antiquated industrial age, hierarchical business model, the modern co-creative workplace is where we experience and learn a variety of relationship skills to succeed. Working in a co-equal circle is a far more evolved interpersonal environment than the pyramid of command and control. Project teams and ad hoc partnerships demand highly developed communication abilities—emotional intelligence, empathic sensitivity and shared leadership—all focused on creative productivity. "Team love" is a unique and new relationship skill to develop, one that requires personal growth and maturation, mindfulness, accountability, and the capacity to balance professionalism and personality.

I subscribe to the legendary Peter Principle whereby workers and executives often get promoted in a company or organization until they reach the level of their incompetence, and that's where they stay. They encounter a ceiling above which they cannot go, and it's usually about people: they don't have the people skills to manage people. It's no wonder that my most successful CEO friend grew up in a family of nine. He learned how to communicate, share, and apply the "five E's" of effective leadership in his work: Engage others, Empathize with them, Educate, Enroll, and Empower. It's not rocket science, but interpersonal savvy and a genuine interest in people, liking and being curious about people, and understanding that we are all here to help each other.

Love Partnership

Are you ready now for some more love—romantic love? If you've done your inner work to become whole, and, through various relationships, learned how to communicate, express your emotions, trust, collaborate, have fun, be a friend, know agape, and love yourself, then you're prepared. But if you desire a love partner, know that it takes energy, time, commitment, focus, change. Love partnerships are complex and uncertain, yet the most fulfilling on all levels. That's why we rush in.

Sustainable love relationships have the synergistic sharing of all parts of ourselves. It takes personal growth, experience, and maturity to achieve this state of being. In a love relationship, do you both energize each other? Are your mind, heart, body, and spirit mutually stimulated?

Before all of that, it takes two whole people choosing to come together to create synergy. The basis for a sustainable relationship, therefore, depends primarily on each person living their own energized wholeness. Co-dependence is not sustainable. Great partnerships are the result of both partners having created their own lives, being self-sufficient, knowing how to live alone, liking themselves, and not being needy.

In this world of choices and possibilities, we get picky. We want just the right person, and if you have lived on your own and established your preferences, interests, habits, and so on, finding somebody who fits into your lifestyle is not all that easy. We like somebody to mirror us, but where can we find that person? And how do you know the person is really right? We are all entertained and drawn to difference and variety, but which ones can we live with, or not? It all gets a bit confusing, consumes energy, and is accompanied by the very real possibility that it can all come crashing down. Is it worthwhile, is it worth the hassle? Yes. Nature tells us to mate. Sexual attraction is basic to our nature. Repression of this strongest of drives obstructs and limits our life-force.

A particularly challenging part of the modern love life is that the traditional rules and roles in relationships have changed. With our new sense of relationship equality, who is what, and who does what? With such lifestyle freedom of expression, it seems like successful dating and partnering is a constant negotiation process of managing differences and preferences: "Do you like this, and do I want that?"

In these times of change, we change, but can our partners adapt, or should they have to? Most of my clients in my counseling practice are women, and their most frequent complaint is that while they are expanding and growing their lives, their spouse or partner is not. Then it's time to redefine the relationship and re-negotiate the terms of its continuance. Again, "re," "re," "re."

I am often asked how to rekindle the fire of a relationship. That's not so easy if you want to reproduce the romantic quality of the initial attraction after you've been together for years. People and partnerships grow and become different, move into a new cycle of relationship with new reasons for being together. That's usually the case and is understandable, but if you really want to reclaim the romance, then you must romance the relationship. Romancing it means knowing how to give it sustainable love. Call upon your sustain-ability to renew and recycle, keep it fresh, change it up. Be creative; don't get into a rut of becoming an old shoe to each other. Rock the boat, be adventurous, do new things together. Have fun.

Romancing your partnership is the way to reinvigorate *eros* love, or sex. Generally, men want sex, but romancing a woman means to romance the relationship, which is far deeper than traditional romancing. It's about growing a relationship by consciously cultivating its synergy and the usual qualities that all

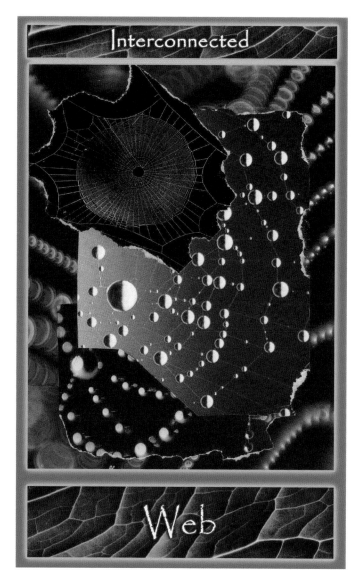

Interconnected

Web

studies of relationships agree upon—emotional intimacy, respect, consideration, constant communication, positive empowerment, shared vision, creating things together. Sustainable sex is the result of a full relationship, a healthy tree of love that grows and grows.

Because we have so many different aspects of ourselves that want satisfaction, it's challenging to find one person to fulfill all of those aspects and keep satisfying them as both people change and grow. Perhaps for some people, non-traditional love relationships would be more sustainable. For the first time in modern history, French women are having more affairs then men. What's that saying? How about the small ethnic group called the Mosuo who live in eastern China near Tibet, who have a matriarchal culture and the custom of "walking marriages"? Among the Mosuo, men and women do not live together, and both can conduct sexual relations with as many partners as they wish. Children are raised by the mother and grandmother. On the nature side, check out the diminutive vole (a kind of mouse) which lives a life of serial monogamy? And how about the highly intelligent and promiscuous dolphins?

Love is complicated and thus, more than anything else, requires constant and honest communication. It is impossible to manage a healthy relationship and sustain yourself throughout your love-life saga without the art of communicating. In fact, all relationships today are more various, more mutable, more complex, and require more communication skills than ever before in human history. We should all be required to take classes in communication, particularly about conflict resolution and non-violent language.

Of all the personal and spiritual growth paths, it seems to me that the art of relating and loving is the highest. And of all the sustain-abilities, coupling demands continuously balancing the most superior of virtues—compassion and passion, empathy and integrity, acceptance and discernment, generosity and boundaries. Love is the most enlivening, orgasmic, enchanting, yet vexing, exasperating, conflicting part of our lives. It can be so juicy and yet so messy. Jump in. It's a big wave, scary and exhilarating. Go for the ride. Isn't that what life is about? It really is true that it's far better to have loved and lost than not to have loved at all.

It has been said, "Only the fool would become wise." Why is that? Because we learn from our experience and we experience from our foolishness. We all make mistakes in love and do foolish things, but have no regrets about the past and project nothing into the future. Maybe it's just all pheromones and chemistry and crazy wicked serendipity, all out of our control. Hooking up is not a business plan. You must trust, be proactive, and in love with life. Do it, engage, and you will be alive and feel alive!

Put your whole heart into it because we are here to love. It takes a tremendous sustain-ability to give it your all, and as we live with love's ambiguity, uncertainty and change, be able to let go, adjust and get back into it. Because of love's tremendous highs and lows, it's a balancing act, and mindful meditation helps you get through and heal any pain and wounding, and handle ecstasy and bliss with equanimity.

Potentiated Love

The sine qua non for sustaining any kind of relationship is to respect and care for another's life path. Compassionate caring is active. Empower others by actively supporting and energizing their growth and evolution. To potentiate a person is an evolved and conscious way to sustain a relationship even though we may disagree and diverge, divorce, and dissolve. This spiritual, life-based, underlying core of connection, friendship and love cannot be broken, regardless of what happens.

I don't know you
but I love you.
I do know you
and I still love you.
I need you
and I encourage you
to be more of you.

Part Six:

SUSTAINABLE WORLD

We often ignore co-evolution—how we, ourselves, evolve with our surroundings—and, according to the tenets of "geo-psychology," our consciousness morphs with the physical area we inhabit. The power of place is profound. It has a major impact on who you are and the life you lead. Being at home in your home, belonging to and participating in some kind of community, and having a healthy Mother Nature are home-base environments that are the rock of our existence—sustain-abilities that we absolutely cannot live without.

12: Home Base

Bees have hives, deer have forests, redwoods have canyons, cactuses have deserts—we all have our habitats. Are you in yours? We often end up in places we'd never choose. Fifty percent of Americans still live within fifty miles of where they grew up. We get lost in cities or live in suburbs that are just places to drive through. Do you live in the climate and community that sustain you? Are you in the right kind of accommodation? Does your neighborhood have the right vibe for you? Do you call Earth home? Are you at home at your home?

Having a home and feeling at home is the bedrock of sustain-ability. With a home base, we have a base camp, a stable rock from which we can launch our lives. Without home, we are, in a way, dismembered and not whole. The same is true without a sense of family. Without a place you can call home, you are living in exile. As in nature, a fish out of water does not live long. Finding your domicile of preference is the foundation of life. Establishing roots enables you to grow a family, circle of friends, perhaps a flourishing business, and provide the stability for realizing your full potential.

Community

Home is certainly more than just an apartment or house; it's the community in which you live. Having a sense of community is primordial, and it's how all living organisms function together in an ecosystem. For many reasons that we all know, the old-fashioned village is a historic relic. Today, virtual communities on the Internet compensate for fragmented townships where there is little contact and trust between actual neighbors.

We are losing physical touch, and we are physical beings with physical instincts and physical needs. We like physical contact and face-to-face communication. Data has shown that interest groups that have come together online and then met in person experience a significant deepening of their relationship. Ninety-eight percent of our human existence has been in a hunter-gatherer culture, so we do have the DNA still within us that is designed for allegiance to a physical gathering place and communal living.

Lack of community is a substantial issue in the degeneration of our society: twenty-five percent of Americans have nobody to talk to. Do something, anything, to contribute to some kind of community. Commune. Isolation, social indifference, apathy, and cynicism are unsustainable traits.

It just may be that super-sized political entities like modern nation-states are unsustainable. In such large collectives, we encounter ethnic, racial, cultural, and ideological differences, which lead to lack of familiarity and trust. Without feelings of allegiance and trust, it's difficult to imagine an ongoing effective union. This is why we see so many large countries splitting apart. Even though there is an efficient economy of scale in largeness, big is probably too big for the human heart that desires and needs communal connection.

Here I am reminded of the adage that "to win, you must participate." As we become more crowded together yet more distant from each other, we turn into a culture of passive spectators sitting on the couch watching somebody else's version of life. We abdicate our social responsibility to determine our lives. Life goes by in an apathetic, vapid existence, and we become "sheeple"—people who meander and get in line with the herd in a kind of collective hypnotic state, and though perhaps complaining, we do nothing.

Realize that according to neuroscience, our immediate intuitions about others are usually wrong, particularly about those of a different ethnicity and race. Though our ancient "neanderthink" brain is naturally suspicious of foreigners, whether we like it or not, we are here to co-evolve, to accept and welcome new and different traits within ourselves that are embodied in all these people we may see as strange. Diversity is one of nature's absolute lynchpins for its sustainability, so trust and befriend "outsiders" in this new world of variety. Communicate to commune and make community.

Mother Nature

Ultimately, even if we have a great job, robust health, excellent relationships, and a sense of community and home, unless the natural environment in which we live is healthy, what difference does it make? It's amazing how many cultures of yesteryear have fallen for ecological reasons, which in turn have brought on

catastrophic war and disease. Shortsighted ignorance and unsustainable thinking and planning are the culprits. Today, we should know better. We know the history, we have the science, so what's going on with us? Human arrogance and disconnection from nature. We try to control nature and separate ourselves from it, and we simply don't respect its overwhelming power and finality.

So, what to do? Be an active guardian against unnatural acts. Do what you can to support a clean, renewable world; for example, avoid using plastic bags that go into the Pacific Ocean "garbage patch" that is now twice the size of Texas. Earth is our home, don't trash it. Not only that, Earth is our lifeline, so we cannot kill it and ourselves with our own poisons. Even if you don't believe in global warming or the toxicity of pesticides, do the right thing, the smart thing, the natural thing and the sustainable thing: stop messing with Mother Nature.

Be proactive in the defense of nature; just keep doing the small things that you can do. Know your three eco-R's: Reduce, Reuse, Recycle. It's like voting: we don't think our vote makes a difference, but it does. More than your one actual vote, the buzz and vibration of your voting intention and conversation have influence on others. I am not thoroughly immersed about the science behind how new trends and revolutions spread through the ether like the "100th monkey" or the "tipping point" or the "morphogenic field," but my intuition says they're true. Now that we know through quantum physics that when we split a molecule and take one part to the other side of the Earth, tweak it, and see an immediate identical movement in the other particle, it makes me a believer in the amazing and invisible phenomenon of synchronicity and our all-pervasive interconnectedness. When something is in the air—a thought, an intention, a word, an action—it's transmittable and receptive. So, simply talking about the environment is helpful and powerful. Little continuous acts and talk do add up, and the more that happens, small numbers grow exponentially (the multiplier effect), and real physical change in the world is unleashed.

Part Seven:
SUSTAINABLE FUTURE

Sustainability is "the way of life," not just a way of life, like a lifestyle or culture. Sustainability is about revering and protecting all species to create and re-create themselves. The way of life is all-inclusive. Its universal principles perpetuate life for all individuals, relationships, businesses, organizations, and groups of all kinds. As the way of life, sustainability maintains not only present life but life in the future.

14: Legacy

One of nature's job descriptions is to reproduce itself to ensure its ongoing survival and success. Maybe that's the highest priority in nature—to preserve itself by creating sustainable conditions so that life can continue.

Sustainable living is not only for us now but for our progeny and, ultimately, for the human species. We are a product of the past and have much to be grateful for. Because of our parents and their parents, we enjoy our lifetime. It's a natural, innate sustain-ability to leave a legacy for ongoing life to prosper and propagate.

However, as a mental species with choices and options, we can neglect and override our natural instincts and inborn imperatives to secure the future, destroying instead of creating, depleting instead of regenerating. We must remember our role on Earth and re-emphasize our future-making responsibility.

Be the Future Now

Nature shows us that when we think ahead about the sustainability of future generations, we live more responsibly and prudently. Nature knows how to live for now and the future, to be eco-nomic and eco-logic without the indulgences, depletions, and waste that poison the future.

When we make a viable future our highest priority, we have the collective motivation and inspiration to desist from narrow, short-term, gluttonous, immediate-gratification behavior. We might vote for new taxes for schools and seek to restore true equality of opportunity in our society. We summon the political will to utilize renewable energy sources and clean up our environmental messes. We could find a way to agree in our polarized society.

So, paradoxically, focusing on a sustainable future is not only good for the future but judicious, sagacious, and imminently practical and worthwhile for the now. Long-term thinking leads us to do things that inherently sustain us well in the present.

Nature shows us that to have a future requires regular and periodic re-calibrations, some of which we might call sacrifices but are actually life-giving. For life to reinvent itself, it must always die. The falling leaves, the setting sun, and the waning moon are all life's means of renewal. Nature prunes back to leap ahead, and recycles to spiral forth. We are no different.

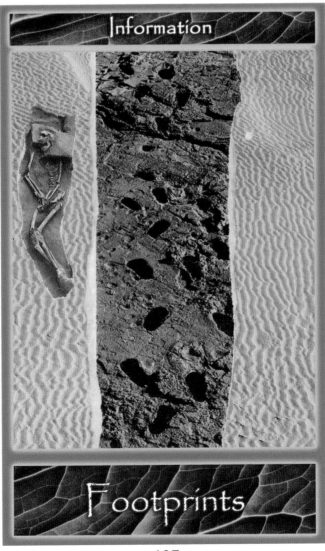

15: Balanced and Conscientious

The sustainable way of life is a balanced life, and taking care of the future naturally brings us back to balance. While not the sexiest of concepts, balance is nevertheless the sustaining genius and force of nature. As my French teacher, M. Aubry, said when he was ninety-seven years young, the key to life is "moderation in all things." The sustain-able path is doing it all—caring for all your parts, as well as others, the Earth, the future. That means you do not overdo any one thing; you are naturally balanced.

If this sounds awfully puritanical, too much work and no fun, that's not true. It's a sustain-ability to enjoy and play but not compromise health and productivity, creativity, and renewability. Look at navigating a balanced life as an art, and love yourself for doing the adept, dexterous, and masterful thing to keep you from capsizing.

To live in balance requires self-awareness, but not deep, constant ruminations (which are too mental, self-doubting, and self-indulgent). Balance-awareness is having a "sense of center"—what you know is balancing or unbalancing you. When we find our center, which is an instinctive/intuitive knowing, we live a more conscientious life of being more responsible, organized, attentive, and caring.

These virtues of conscientiousness have been identified as the best predictors of those who live the healthiest and longest, according to the monumental study called "The Longevity Project" by Howard S. Friedman and Leslie R. Martin. Over eight decades, the same 1,500 people were tracked (there's no other research like this) and the conscientious, prudent, and thrifty people sustained the best. It's no coincidence that these are the very same qualities of nature.

This study also declares that "modern medicine has relatively little to offer for your optimal path to health and longevity." Other studies have also found that the best doctor is you. If you are in pain, instead of taking Vicodin, the most widely sold drug in America, go within: recent neuroscience research has proven that the power of the mind—engaging in activities such as meditation and immersion in mental endeavors—is most effective.

16: Spirit of Sustainability

We began this book with sustainability as the "new success" and this journey has taken us to the other end of the spectrum, which is sustainability as a spiritual path.

At its most basic level, sustainability means perpetuating the mysterious force that gives us life. It's making the life-force sacred, and the ultimate source of renewal. This spirituality has no elaborate set of beliefs other than to revere life and follow the natural eco-principles of life. For my own version of worshipping the divine, nature is my church and sustainability is my religion.

According to surveys, having some kind of spiritual path promotes a healthier lifestyle. Studies find that spiritual people exhibit fewer self-destructive behaviors, have less stress, and greater total life satisfaction.

The spirit of sustainability is enhanced by making it a spiritual practice. Why not do a conscious sustain-ability action every day. For my practice and perhaps for you, I have created a published deck of sustainability cards—Sustain Yourself Cards—101 nature collages representing our sustain-abilities that include the elements, natural phenomena, minerals, plants, animals, and humans. Each day I pick a card that suggests what Mother Nature wants to tell me about sustaining myself. I take action on this Earth's wisdom. It's fun, intuitive, inspiring, and keeps you focused on this Earth-walk of ours.

Sustain on!

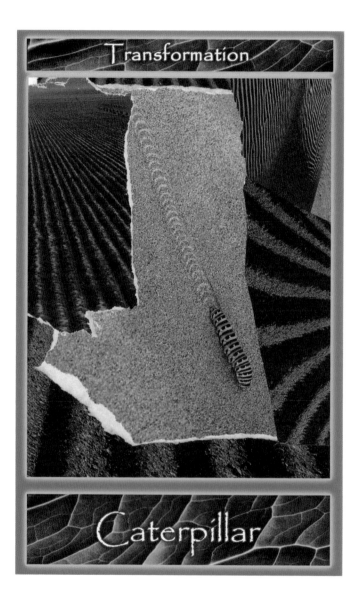

Transformation

Caterpillar

Part Eight:
THE SUSTAIN-ABILITY GYM

Take this personal inventory to determine how sustain-able you are. The way of sustainability requires self-awareness; these questions will help you become more conscious, conscientious, and motivated.

The intention of the Sustain-Ability Gym is to get fit for life by exercising your sustain-abilities to become more sustainable. Because nature is active and gets results, take one action per question. Sometimes the action is mental. Sometimes it's speaking to yourself. Having a "sustainability buddy" to work with is the most effective way to ensure accountability.

You can use this inventory as your Sustainability Action Journal.

INTENTION

Give five reasons why you want to Sustain Yourself:

SOURCES OF SUSTAINABILITY

What's your primary source of sustainability?
Action:

1. THE NEW SUCCESS

How do you feel successful about your life?
Action:

What aspect of your success is sustain-able?
Action:

What part of your success is not sustain-able?
Action:

2. THE SUSTAINABILITY IMPERATIVE

Why do you want to be more sustain-able?
Action:

What motivates you to have the sustainable life?
Action:

DEPLETION
How do you deplete yourself?
Action:

What's your favorite "re" word?
Action:

What wave of life moves you?
Action:

How are you not authentic?
Action:

WASTE
What have you wasted in your life?
Action:

What talents have you unused or underused?
Action:

How have you undervalued yourself?
Action:

TOXICITY
How do you pollute yourself with critical thoughts?
Action:

3. NATURE KNOWS HOW

What part of Nature makes you feel good?
Action:

What part of Nature do you most identify with?
Action:

How do you live naturally?
Action:

4. WHOLE AND HEALTHY

How healthy are you?
Action:

Mental Health?
Action:

Emotional health?
Action:

Physical health?
Action:

Spiritual health?
Action:

Work health?
Action:

Relationships health?
Action:

Social health?
Action:

Environmental health?
Action:

How often do you go into Nature for natural health?
Action:

What change in the world do you need to make within yourself?
Action:

5. CHANGE-ABLE

What do you need to "re"?
Action:

Are you changing?
Action:

ADAPTING
How are you adapting?
Action:

What did you do today that was new?
Action:

GROWING
How are you growing?
Action:

How are you growing a better quality of life?
Action:

What Inner Potentials are you growing?
Action:

What outer resources are you developing?
Action:

What situations are you expanding?
Action:

What New growth in the world is your growth opportunity?
Action:

GROWTH TREE
SEED
What parts of your DNA seed do you want to change?
Action:.

What are you seeking in yourself?
Action:

ROOTS
How rooted are you?
Action:

Are you rooted in a sustainable environment?
Action:

TRUNK
What's your present focus in life?
Action:

BRANCHES
How are you branching out?
Action:

FALLING LEAVES
What are you letting go?
Action:

FRUITS
What is your fruition?
Action:

What harvest are you reaping?
Action:

How is your flowering part of your destiny?
Action

SLOW GROWTH
What are you growing slowly?
Action:

How are you being patient and persevering?
Action:

BARK
How do you protect yourself?
Action:

RECYCLING
What season of the life cycle are you in?
Action:

How are you Recycling yourself?
Action:

BREAKING-THROUGH
How are you breaking out?
Action:

What small changes are you making to prepare for breaking through?
Action:

6. CREATIVE MIND

How creative a thinker are you?
Action:

MENTAL HEALTH
How positive are you?
Action:

Do you believe in yourself, no doubts?
Action:

Are you open and opportunistic?
Action:

How do you re-frame your language?
Action:

INTUITION
Do you trust your intuitions?
Action:

How do your intuitions come to you?
Action:

Do you have the courage to act on your intuition?
Action:

Do you catch yourself projecting your own thoughts, emotions, motivations onto others?
Action:

How are you authentic and original?
Action:

Are you curious and learning?
Action:

Do you use your imagination?
Action:

Do you catch yourself thinking catastrophically?
Action:

Do you use your whole brain of imagination and logic?
Action:

7. HEART OF MOTIVATION

Are you complacent?
Action:

How are you motivated?
Action:

How expressive are you of your emotions?
Action:

Do you a heart vision?
Action:

Do you enjoy the present?
Action:

How happy are you?
Action:

Do you laugh?
Action:

What wave of emotion are you riding?
Action:

How do you maintain emotional balance?
Action:

8. RENEWABLE BODY

Do your keep your body moving and exercise?
Action:

Do you go outside into the natural light?
Action:

How do you do your aerobics?
Action:

Do you make sounds and sound out?
Action:

Do you drink enough water?
Action:

Do you eat healthy?
Action:

Do you go barefoot on the earth?
Action:

How do you sleep?
Action:

Are you neotenous?
Action:

How renewable is your body?
Action:

9. INSPIRED LIFE OF DESTINY

Do you know yourself?
Action:

Do you do what you know?
Action:

Do you know your Path of Destiny?
Action:

What's your mind's eye picture of it?
Action:

Do you believe your Heart Vision?
Action:

What actions are you taking to live your destiny?
Action:

What results are you getting on your path?
Action:

How do you let your destiny pull you along?
Action:

What old self-identity are you letting go of?
Action:

How inspired are you?
Action:

10. SYNERGY!

Are you energetic?
Action:

How is your mind energized?
Action:

How energized are you emotionally?
Action:

How energized are you physically?
Action:

How are you synergized (your mind, heart, body, spirit)?
Action:

How are you synergized with your work?
Action:

How are you synergized with your relationships?
Action:

How are you synergized with your lifestyle?
Action:

Do you express your energies in the world?
Action:

What are you attracting to you?
Action:

How do you conserve your energy?
Action:

How do you use the positive use of "No"?
Action:

11. SUSTAINABLE WORK

How are you productive?
Action:

Do you have right livelihood?
Action:

Are you symbiotic with your work?
Action:

How is your work or your profession?
Action:

Is your work profitable?
Action:

How is your work growth path?
Action:

How is your work your life purpose?
Action:

How is your work your passion?
Action:

How playful is your work?
Action:

What does the future of work look like for you?
Action:

How are you a solopreneur?
Action:

How do you collaborate?
Action:

How well do you communicate?
Action:

How empathic are you?
Action:

How are you growing your business?
Action:

12. SUSTAINABLE LOVE

How do you love life?
Action:

Connection Love
How do you make friends?
Action:

How do you like people?
Action:

Can you say, "I don't know you, but I love you"?
Action:

What aspect of nature are you in touch with?
Action:

Self-Love
How do you love yourself?
Action:

What have you learned about yourself from relationships?
Action:

How do you project yourself onto others?
Action:

What shadow side of you are you working on?
Action:

How are you growing yourself?
Action:

How giving are you to others?
Action:

Inter-Dependent Love

SUSTAINABLE LIFE

How do you create inter-dependence with others?
Action:

How do you compete with others?
Action:

Belonging Love
What allegiances do you have?
Action:

What groups do you feel like you belong to?
Action:

Family Love
How do you have some kind of family in your life?
Action:

How expressive of emotions are you with others?
Action:

How do you have fun with others?
Action:

How trusting are you of others?
Action:

How do you relate to your family of origin?
Action:

How do you relate to your family of choice:
Action:

Teamwork Love
How do you relate in teams?
Action:

128

How do you do the Five E's? (Engage others, Empathize with them, Educate, Enroll, and Empower)
Action:

Love Partnership
Do you have a love relationship?
Action:

If not, do you desire a love partner?
Action:

How do you and your love partner synergize each other?
Action:

How independent are you?
Action:

How do you adapt to the changing roles in your relationships?
Action:

How do you handle the ambiguities and uncertainties of love?
Action:

How are you able to redefine and renegotiate partnerships?
Action:

How do you have romance partnerships?
Action:

How healthy are your sexual relations?
Action:

What other forms of partnerships have you considered?
Action:

How are you as a communicator?
Action:

Are you a relationship risk-taker?
Action:

How do you maintain emotional balance in partnerships?
Action:

POTENTIATED LOVE

How do you potentiate another?
Action:

13. HOME BASE

Is where you live home?
Action:

Do you live in the right community for you?
Action:

Do you live in the right natural environment for you?
Action:

Do you commune (contribute to a community)?
Action:

Are you open to strangers?
Action:

How do you protect our natural environment?
Action:

Do you Reduce, Reuse, Recycle?
Action:

14. LEGACY

How grateful are you to your forebears?
Action:

How are you contributing to the future?
Action:

How does ensuring the future help you now?
Action:

What do you need to sacrifice to live?
Action:

15. BALANCED AND CONSCIENTIOUS

How are you balanced?
Action:

What unbalances you?
Action:

What can you do to re-balance yourself?
Action:

How are you conscientious?
Action:

How do you become unconscious?
Action:

16. SPIRIT OF SUSTAINABILITY

How do you have a path of spirituality?
Action:

How do you perpetuate the life-force?
Action:

How does your spiritual path help you be sustainable?
Action:

Color

Rainbow

About the Author

James Wanless, Ph.D. (Political Science, Columbia University) is an internationally recognized author, keynoter, educator, futurist and consultant. Pioneer of new thinking and a lifestyle trail-blazer, he is recognized for weaving ageless wisdom into modern life. His latest book, *Sustainable Life: The New Success*, guides you along a revolutionary path towards living a whole life, becoming truly self-sustaining, personally and professionally.

Wanless, aka "Greening Man," has recently created a deck of green wisdom, eco-cards entitled *Sustain Yourself Cards and Handbook to Live Well and Live Long*. This tool for creative insight and inspiration shows his own colorful art of nature and has been used by companies like Oracle and Boeing and human potential centers in China and Europe.

This dynamic speaker and trainer is a noted authority on intuition for right brain innovation, decision-making and communication. James is the creator of the best-selling *Voyager Intuition Cards*, and the author of several books, including

Intuition@Work (RedWheel/Weiser); *The Way of the Great Oracle* for designing the future; and One Spirit Book-of-the-Month Club selection, *Strategic Intuition for the 21st Century* (Harmony).

Wanless has recently released "The Fortune Formula", a CD of guided meditations on the golden rules of manifestation. He is presently working on his next book, *The Fortune Formula for Living the Fortune Life.*

Wanless is an active online presence with websites www.SustainYourselfCards.com, www.VoyagerTarot.com, Intuition podcasts on iTunes, various YouTube presentations, Facebook, Twitter, and other social networks.

With his magical blend of personal charisma, humor, and pragmatic enthusiasm, this enthusiastic explorer of consciousness engages audiences in a transformative experience that inspires and enlightens.

The Living Future

We hope you
enjoyed this book. For
more ideas and resources to create
a sustainable life and a sustainable
world, we invite you to visit our
website at:

www.TheLivingFuture.org

21071818R00076